The Valley of Decision

The Valley of Decision

By Major Mitchell

Shalakopress.com

The Valley of Decision

All rights reserved
Copyright 2020 Major Mitchell

This is a work of fiction.
All characters and events portrayed in this book are
Fictional, and any resemblance to real people is purely
coincidental.

Reproduction in any manner, in whole or part,
In English or in other language, or otherwise without written
permission of publisher is prohibited.

For information contact: Shalako Press
P.O. Box 371, Oakdale, CA 95371

Printing History
First Printing 2020

ISBN: 978-1-7340795-3-1

PRINTED IN THE UNITED STATES OF AMERICA

ACKNOWLEDGMENTS

This book is a combined effort of many people. I would first like to thank my nephews, Craig Tutorow and Kenneth Mitchell, our son Mark Mitchell, and Brice Brink for their input. Having never been a part of the military I would have made many more mistakes than I already have.

I would like to thank Karen Borrelli for her expertise in designing a great cover for this book. The cover photo was provided by *Fabrizio Conti* on *Unsplash*.

I would like to thank my wife Judy, whose expert editing always turns my hieroglyphics into something readable. Thanks Kid.

I would most of all like to thank each and every reader. It is you after all, the ones who buy our books, who keep us writing.

God bless.

Prologue

A mountain road somewhere in Afghanistan

"You're headin' home, aren't you, ma'am?"

First Lieutenant Cynthia Ann Quentero studied Sergeant Waterman as the Humvee they were riding in crept through a deep rut. A bead of sweat mapped its way from beneath her helmet, down her left cheek and to her chin. They were officially moving medical supplies from Bagram Air Base to Kandahar, but the real cargo was the two high-profile prisoners handcuffed inside the truck directly behind the Humvee she was riding in. They were traveling under the cloak of darkness, hoping to slip past any Islamic terrorist that might want the prisoners back.

This was Waterman's first tour and he had been talking non-stop since they had entered the mountains. The narrow road would have been dangerous regardless, but al Qaeda and the Islamic State deemed the prisoners and cargo they were carrying to be worth their weight in gold.

Cynthia smiled at the young sergeant seated across from her. He was cradling his M-4 between his knees with the barrel pointed toward the floor. His uniform had sweat stains that seemed to grow larger by the minute.

"Yes," she said.

"When?"

"Next Tuesday."

"Okay, let's stop the chatter," Captain Miller said as he surveyed the blackness of the Afghan night through the window. "We're in enemy territory and I want everyone alert."

Cynthia gave the sergeant a nod before turning to stare through her window. There were sweat stains growing on her uniform also, only smaller and slower. She could remember when her uniform looked worse than Waterman's. She'd heard from well-seasoned soldiers that when you ceased being nervous and afraid about going into battle, it was time to go home. People who aren't afraid and who don't respect their enemy take chances and make mistakes that will get someone hurt or killed. She tugged unconsciously at her shirt, next to her Marine Military Police insignia.

She caught her breath and yelled as a bright flash appeared on the hill.

"Incoming!"

The front of the lead Humvee exploded into flames with a deafening bang.

"Delta Five-One is hit," she yelled as they piled out of the Humvee opposite the hillside.

"Anyone see where that came from?" Captain Miller yelled.

"Top of the hill, sir," Cynthia shouted above the din as the soldiers returned gunfire.

She yelled again as another flash from the hill caused the front of the rear Humvee to explode, stranding the remaining vehicles in the middle.

She studied the hillside as a hail of bullets rattled loudly against the Humvees. *Oh, my God!* The top of the hill was crawling with al Qaeda, working their way downhill and toward them.

Captain Miller cursed loudly and barked orders as he ran back and forth, checking on the rest of the convoy. "Delta Five-eight is hit. Move! Move!"

"Sir...," she started but turned to grab at Waterman as the young sergeant dropped his rifle and darted toward the lead vehicle. The rear door of the Humvee had swung open and a soldier fell out with the back of his uniform on fire. Waterman tackled the soldier as he tried to run and smothered the flames with his own jacket.

"Welcome to Afghanistan," Cynthia mumbled. She quickly turned as Captain Miller fell next to her feet with a blank stare.

"Sir! Sir! Talk to me, sir!" She cradled his head in her hands and slapped his face. Receiving no response, she laid his head on the ground and yelled. "Medic! Medic! Captain Miller's down." Two men wearing medical insignias rushed to start working on the fallen captain.

Cynthia glanced at her hands and wiped them against her pant-legs as she ran hunched over. They were covered with Captain Miller's blood. Another hail of bullets rattled against the Humvee. She yelled at the men behind the neighboring Humvee.

"We have contact right-left. Move! Move! Henderson, Jackson. Get the .50 Cal and 240 rocking. Give us some cover. Fire!"

The two soldiers scrambled onto the backs of separate Humvees and begin firing the heavy machine guns.

"And you," she yelled at a soldier guarding the prisoners. "If they try to escape … shoot them!"

"Yes, ma'am," he said and racked a round into the chamber of his M4.

She fired a couple of quick bursts from the rear of the Humvee, and then darted forward to the front of the vehicle bent over. Catching her breath, she saw a rebel armed with an RPG scramble closer to the convoy. Raising her rifle, she lowered it again as a burst from Jackson's .50 caliber machine gun knocked him backward.

"Good shooting, Jackson!"

She crawled to the opened Humvee door and grabbed the microphone.

"We have contact Delta Five. One and eight hit! Request air support! We're taking massive casualties!"

A second later the radio came alive.

"Copy Delta Five. We have air support in your area approximately five mikes out. Send coordinates."

She cringed as a bullet ricocheted off the neighboring Humvee and whined dangerously close.

"Delta, this is Delta Five-Two. We are at 42S – 4268170200. Enemy is 200 yards north on top of the ridge line."

"Copy Delta Five, Bandit, mike out."

Please God...hurry. She had no more gotten the prayer from her lips when the radio crackled again.

"Delta Five, this is Bandit. We're on scene and engaging target."

Thank you, Jesus, she said as the sound of an Apache helicopter drew closer. She clicked her microphone once more.

"Copy Bandit, take them out!"

Cynthia scrambled back to the left front fender. The helicopter sounded right on them now. Sergeant Waterman had the wounded soldier across his shoulders and was headed her way. He made it halfway when he fell, holding his left leg.

Come on, God. Get us outa here.

She leaned her M4 against the Humvee and dashed toward Waterman, sliding to his side like a baseball player.

"Take Patterson," Waterman said. "He's hurt pretty bad."

She grabbed the unconscious soldier's arm and dragged him toward the Humvee, where she passed him off to the medics. Turning quickly, she scrambled back to Waterman, who was making an effort to crawl back on his own.

"Here," she grabbed his arm around her shoulder, "you wait much longer and you'll be shaking their hands." She half ran, dragging him to the vehicle as the Apache came into view. The radio crackled with the pilot's voice.

"We have a visual on Tango."

The darkness lit up like noonday sun as the Apache

fired a burst from its M230 chain gun. The top of the hill exploded into a cloud of dust and gravel as the automatic cannon released its 30 mm projectiles at a rate of 625 rounds per minute. Cindy dropped Waterman at the medic's feet and leaned against the Humvee gasping for breath as the Apache fired several more bursts.

The radio came alive once more. "Delta, this is Bandit. You're clear. Let's go home."

She yelled. "Come on, you heard the man. Let's mount up, or we'll be late for dinner." The soldiers scrambled inside the vehicles with a shout. Cindy helped get Patterson inside her Humvee then pushed against Waterman as they pulled him inside. She glanced around quickly then yelled at Waterman "What about the others?"

"They're all dead. Let's get out of here."

She could taste bile as she clicked on her microphone.

"What about the rear?"

"We're banged up, but all accounted for."

"Then make sure we've got everyone and let's go home."

She handed Waterman her M4 and had one boot on the running board when a single rebel appeared from behind a rock 50 yards to her left. He fired a spray of bullets as she stepped up. "Oh God," she cried as a bullet slammed into her lower back, knocking her half-way into the vehicle. She tried grabbing her footing as she slid backward but nothing seemed to work

Waterman grabbed her wrist and yelled, "Help me!" Another soldier crawled over Captain Miller's body to help pull her inside.

Cindy could hear the gun on the Apache as it eliminated the rebel who had shot her. Someone slammed the door closed as the Humvee lurched forward. A large black man with a medical insignia rolled her on her side and pulled her shirt up.

"How bad is it, Gary?"

"You've got a nasty hole near your spine. Does that hurt?"

"I thought I'd gotten hit with a ball bat, but now? I don't feel a thing. Why?"

"No reason. I'm packing a clot on your back, so try not to move."

"How's Captain Miller?"

"He didn't make it."

She rolled her head to see the covered body, and then raised her hand to salute him.

"Hold still or you'll be joining him."

Cindy listened quietly as the Humvee rocked and banged its way around the stranded lead vehicle. One explosion, followed by a second explosion a minute later, told her that neither of the crippled Humvees would provide the enemy with anything useful. She heard the medic scold Waterman for not holding still as he tried packing gauze pads with a clotting agent against his leg. She tried to move her own legs again, but felt nothing. She did, however, feel Sergeant Waterman as he held one of her hands and started praying for her. *That was nice.*

She could hear the radio inside the Humvee as the Apache drew overhead.

"Delta, this is Bandit. We're bingo plus 10."

Ten minutes of fuel left? That's cutting it kind of close, Bandit.

The driver's voice cracked as he answered back. "Copy that, Bandit. Thanks for the assist. We owe you a big one."

The whop, whop, whop of the helicopter blades faded and the co-driver began communicating with the base in code. "Roger, nine line as follows, break. One, Tango-alpha 6577, break. Two, 39.39, E-7-Romeo, break. Three, 1, Alpha 1, 2, 2 Charlie, break."

Cynthia closed her eyes and tried to pray. The driver was requesting a medical airlift among other things.

I wonder how many were wounded. At least mine

doesn't hurt; I can thank you for that, God. If it doesn't hurt, it can't be too bad, can it?

Cynthia slowly lost consciousness as the Humvee wound its way downhill.

Chapter 1

One year later – Modesto, CA.

Cynthia expertly guided her wheelchair down the long hallway, pausing every now and then to read the nameplates fastened to the doors. She stopped two-thirds of the way and smiled at her reflection in the window next to a door marked *Peter Fowler, M.D. General Practice*. She was dressed pretty much the same when they said goodbye two years earlier when she was home on leave. She was wearing Marine camouflage then too, minus the wheelchair, of course.

Peter Fowler had been one of her closest and dearest friends. They had known each other since kindergarten. After both her parents were killed in a head-on auto accident caused by a drunken driver, she and her brother Bobby moved into the Fowler's ranch house and became part of the family. Peter's parents became her parents, and his sister became her sister also. She grinned, remembering how big of a crush she had carried for Peter all through school. She even dreamed of them getting married after graduation, but he never gave any indication of feeling the same toward her. After graduation, Peter enrolled in medical school and she joined the Marines, hoping to eventually become a police officer like her brother. That was almost ten years ago. Bobby was one of Modesto's finest police officers, and Peter had started his residency, and *she* was in a wheelchair.

Cindy was reaching for the handicap button to open the door when a teenage boy on a pair of crutches with a cast on one leg opened the door from inside.

"Oh, let me hold the door for you." He almost fell trying to be nice.

"Thank you," Cindy said with a smile as she entered the reception room. The handicap door buttons all have a thirty-second delay, but the kid was trying to be helpful, so she gave him kudos for being nice.

She stopped in the middle of the waiting area to take it all in. She had visited the office on her last visit home, and the place hadn't changed a bit that she could tell. Oh yeah, she was sure there were newer magazines, maybe only six months old instead of two years, but the white walls and artwork were exactly the same.

The receptionist, Rhonda Tyson, placed the telephone back into the cradle and bounced out of her chair with a squeal.

"Cindy Quentero!" She left her post and came around the registration counter to give Cindy a hug and a kiss on the cheek. "I haven't seen you in what...?"

"Two years, six months and 14 days," Cindy said. "Since I was home on leave."

"Well, how are you doing, honey?" Rhonda took a step back to take Cindy in.

"I'm doing pretty good, considering. I'm learning to drive one of these things." She patted the arm of the wheelchair. "They don't come with instructions."

"No, I guess they don't."

Rhonda crossed the room to open a door just a crack.

"Dr. Fowler, Miss Quentero is here for her two o'clock appointment."

"Tell her I'll be right with her." His voice floated through the door.

He sounds the same.

The Valley of Decision

"I was sorry to hear you got shot and that you're in that thing," Rhonda said as she returned to Cindy's side, "but it's good to see you again. We all missed you."

The examination room door opened and a blond-headed two-year-old licking a sucker trailed his mother into the lobby. They were followed by an attractive man in his late thirties, dressed in a white lab coat.

"Even Dr. Fowler?" Cindy said with a grin.

"Especially Dr. Fowler," Rhonda said with a firm nod.

Dr. Fowler grinned as he crossed the room and stood beside her chair to study her with his hands on his hips.

"The medical profession suffered when you joined the Marines. Up 'til then someone had to drive you here at least once a week to get you pieced back together."

He took the chair by the handles and pushed it toward the examination room.

"Mmm...I wasn't quite that bad. And that was mostly from working at your dad's cattle ranch."

"And riding in rodeos," Peter added with a chuckle.

The nurse held the door to the examination room open as they entered. Cindy scrunched her brow as she stared at her.

"Becky? I know you're his sister, but isn't it a little much having to work with him all day?"

Becky laughed as she closed the door. "He's mellowed a lot and gotten easier to tolerate."

"She forgets who signs the timecards around here. Now..." he sat on a stool with rollers and stared thoughtfully. "I heard from Mom and Dad that you were released from the V.A. hospital a couple of weeks ago. What did the V.A. say, and how can I help?"

Cindy reached into a pouch attached to the wheelchair and handed him a thick envelope.

"Here's my records, for what they're worth. They say the bullet damaged my spine and I'll be stuck in this thing 'til I die and go to heaven."

"It could be," he said, cocking his head with raised eyebrows. "How do you feel about that?"

"I'm a Marine, Pete. We don't know the meaning of defeat. I want to get back on my feet, no matter what it takes."

Dr. Fowler grinned. "I thought you being born a Quentero would have been enough to accomplish that. Lean as far forward as you can."

Cindy leaned over, bracing her elbows against her knees. Dr. Fowler lifted her shirt in back and pressed on the scar. "It looks like it's healing nicely. Can you feel anything?"

Cindy shook her head. "Nope, not a thing. Only pressure."

"You feel pressure?"

"Yeah, but more like being pushed forward. It feels like everything's asleep."

Dr. Fowler swung the stool around and began typing on the computer. "That's better than I thought. At least you're able to feel something. I'm not promising anything, but I want to see you back here next Tuesday at 10:00 am. It'll give me time to study your records and talk to a colleague who knows about spinal injuries. Is your phone number and address up to date in the file?"

"Ah, no, I'll give my cell number to Rhonda before I leave. I've been crashing at Bobby's house, but it's small and they have two kids. I'm looking for my own place."

Dr. Fowler nodded with a crooked grin.

"Problem solved. You can stay at the ranch. How is your brother doing?"

"Bobby's fine, but don't you think your mom and dad might have something to say about me moving in there? And what about Becky and Seth? I think you guys have already put up with me long enough."

"Seth only cares about horses and trucks, and Becky moved into town with me."

"We're splitting the payments on a three-bedroom near the hospital," Becky said as Cindy's eyes danced between the two.

"Besides," Peter said, "you and Bobby both lived with us almost ten years after your parents died. I'll bet he still knows every inch of the ranch." He scooted the stool back in front of Cindy and smiled. "Mom will be in heaven having you there. She still thinks you're her daughter, you know. She cried for a week when you joined the Marines and went off to war."

He grinned and typed some more into the computer.

"She started redecorating your old bedroom when we heard you were heading home," Becky said with a chuckle. "Dad and Seth built a handicap ramp for your chair. Everyone's expecting you to live there."

"No, I can't do that. I'd just get in the way. I'll think of something."

"Not if you know what's good for you." Peter laughed.

"You know how Mom is when she's ticked off."

"Yeah," Cindy gave a nod, "but none of you know what it's like living with a disabled vet. I need to talk to her before doing anything. I still feel like it'll get old real quick when I start having flashbacks and clunking around the house in my chair.

Peter cocked one of his eyebrows. "You won't have time to clunk around in your chair. If you think Becky and I are going to let you lay around getting fat and bored, you've got another think coming, Lieutenant Quentero."

He studied her quietly for a second.

"In the meantime, you need to figure out what God wants you to do, even if it's from that chair. Evidently, he's not done with you yet."

Cindy snorted. "He's got a funny way of showing it. We lost three good men that night."

"True, but you're still here." Peter moved the stool closer and held one of her hands. "What is it that God has planned for Cynthia Quentero?"

"I don't know," Cindy said, shaking her head. "I really don't know."

Chapter 2

Cynthia wheeled her chair back the way she had come toward a large waiting room. She punched the automatic door button a little harder than necessary and wheeled herself inside. Her brother, dressed in a policeman's uniform, grabbed his three-year-old daughter as she bolted toward Cynthia yelling, "Aunt Cindy!"

"That's okay, Bobby. I'll hold her." She held her arms toward the wiggling girl. "I'm sorry that took so long. Pete wanted to talk."

Karen flipped her long blond hair over one shoulder before slipping their six-month-old boy, Robert Jr., into the carrier.

"What did he say?" Karen asked.

"Not much. He wants me back next Tuesday after he reads my file and talks to another doctor."

"No problem," Robert said. "One of us will make sure you get here." He bent over to scold Jennifer as she bounced in Cindy's lap and kissed her Aunt Cindy repeatedly.

"That's okay, Bobby. I need my Jenny fix," Cindy said, nuzzling her niece on the neck and making her giggle.

Robert pushed the door button and took hold of the wheelchair. He wheeled it smoothly into the open where a small crowd had gathered near the Memorial Hospital sign. She stared at the well-dressed man making a speech about crime in front of a television crew with a camera and microphone.

"Isn't that Curtis Roberts?" Cindy asked. "What's he doing?"

"Oh, I guess you didn't hear about him in Afghanistan. The real-estate company he started got into a jam over some legal thing I don't understand. Of course he's claiming it was everyone's fault but his. Now, he's decided to go into politics," Karen said.

"Really? I guess that fits—politicians and something illegal. Last time I talked to him was when he asked me to dance at our graduation party. He said he couldn't wait to leave Modesto."

"Well, that's all changed now and he seems to turn up at the strangest places."

"Like the hospital sign?"

"Exactly."

"I for one wish he'd stayed in L.A." Bobby said, making a wide path around the crowd. "He's starting to be a pain...always pumping me for information. I wish he'd just give up," Robert said with a low growl.

"That's not going to happen." Karen giggled. "He's never given up since I've known him."

"Like I said, this is the first time I've seen him since graduation," Cindy said with a laugh. "Seeing you and Pete, and now him—it's kinda like attending a high school reunion."

A tall well-dressed brunette wearing a headset was busy skirting the edge of the crowd. She stopped to stare at them as Robert tried slipping past her on their way to the parking garage.

"That's Elizabeth Sparks." Karen leaned toward Cindy and raised her voice to be heard over Curtis' booming voice. "She's a local news reporter."

Elizabeth studied Cindy a few seconds longer before waving to get Curtis' attention and direct him toward Cindy and Robert's family. Curtis glanced their way, and then rushed toward them.

"This is a surprise," Curtis said, cutting off their escape. "These are my good friends, Robert Quentero and his family. This is the first time I have seen his sister Cynthia since she joined the service and got wounded in Afghanistan."

He smiled at Robert. "Being a police officer, Robert, what can you tell us about the gang-related shooting last night?"

Robert shook his head and started inching the chair forward.

"No comment. It's under investigation."

Curtis followed with the microphone as Robert tried to guide Karen and the children past Curtis and the camera crew.

"Perhaps you can tell us what is currently being done to combat crime in our neighborhoods."

"Not now, Curt." He tried stepping around Curtis, only to be cut off by Elizabeth and the cameraman. After receiving an angry glare from Robert, Curtis quickly turned toward Cindy.

"On a different subject, perhaps Cynthia can tell us quickly how she is doing?"

Cynthia smiled and eased her chair forward as Curtis and the camera crew followed.

"There's not really a whole lot to tell. I am doing about as well as can be expected."

"Perhaps you might share your views on crime in our neighborhoods?"

"I just arrived home a couple of weeks ago. I really don't have an opinion other than Modesto seems peaceful, compared to Afghanistan."

She grinned at him. "I'm doing fine, really. And Bobby's got to get to work. Maybe later."

She brushed past Curtis and the cameraman to join Robert and Karen at the edge of the crowd. They could still hear Curt as they made their way toward their car.

"For those who may not know Cynthia Quentero's story, Lieutenant Quentero volunteered to go to Afghanistan and serve her country. Her brother, Robert, stayed home and became one of Modesto's finest policemen. As a way of saying thank you to our local heroes, I am asking for your vote this coming October. Help me make our streets safe again."

Karen buckled Jennifer into her car seat while Robert helped Cindy slide from the wheelchair and into the front passenger seat. He then placed the wheelchair in the trunk and slid behind the steering wheel.

They fastened their seat belts as Robert started the metallic green Mustang and placed the car in reverse.

"He might as well give up. He's been trailing Walters in the polls ever since he started campaigning for office."

"Curt won't ever admit he's losing at anything. He never has," Karen said.

"Since when did you guys become his *good friends*?" Cynthia said.

Robert looked over his shoulder as he backed out of his parking stall.

"We're civil, but not close, and we never hung out together. He runs in a different circle than us, just like in high school, and I don't like the people he hangs out with."

Robert started the car forward.

"Well, I've heard that he's changed," Karen said. "Carol told me Curt has started going to church, and she's heard him lead in prayer several times."

"That'd be a switch," Cindy said.

"And I happen to agree with what he's been saying about the gang violence," Karen said.

"I didn't say I disagreed," Robert said. "I get to see it up close and personal. But, I've seen him around town, and I know some of the things he's done. I also know some of the shady business deals his father's pulled. I don't think he's too different from the old man. I simply don't trust him."

"Well...," Karen drug out her words. "People do change, you know."

"Why are you defending him?"

"I'm not defending him. I just said maybe you should give him a chance."

"Besides," Cindy said with a crooked grin, "Karen and I both dated him at one time or the other."

The crease between Robert's eyes deepened as he stared at Cindy.

"I knew about you, but took that as maybe my sister wasn't too bright. But, Karen, my own wife? Nah, I didn't know about that."

"That was when I was a junior in high school, and I only went out with him twice. And how we got on that subject, I don't have a clue. All I said was, give the guy a chance before you throw him under the bus."

"Well, I hope he *has* changed," Robert said with a snort.

Cindy chuckled as the car pulled out onto the street.

"Yeah, let's hope so."

******

Zoe Shultz studied her reflection in the mirror as she inserted the fourth nose ring and nodded. It complimented her orange hair that was almost shaved on one side and spiked on the other half. The white pancake makeup made her black lipstick and eyeliner pop. She adjusted her blouse to hide as much skin as possible, and yet highlight her multiple tattoos. She had long ago decided getting dressed in the morning was a form of art, drawing attention without inviting unwanted advances.

She pulled a few dollars for lunch money and gasoline for her car from the hiding spot taped under one of the dresser drawers and opened her bedroom door. Her mother was passed out on the sofa with the television blaring with a half-empty vodka bottle lying on the floor. Zoe heaved a sigh as she shut the television off and screwed the cap tight on the bottle before setting it on the cluttered coffee table. She tried to slip past Carl, her mother's latest boyfriend, who she thought was passed out on the floor until he grabbed her leg and attempted to run his hand up toward her crotch.

"Agh, you slug!" She jerked away and kicked at him.

"Aw, come on. You know you want me."

"In your dreams."

She slammed the front door and ran for the car as Carl stuck his head out the door. "Come back, Zoe. I'll show you what it's like to be with a real man."

"That certainly wouldn't be you," she yelled back. The old Chevy started with a cloud of smoke and she pulled away from the curb wishing Carl Mongrove was dead and rotting in hell.

Chapter 3

Elizabeth Sparks arrived at the studio fifteen minutes late for work. After placing her purse into the bottom drawer, she sipped her latte as she studied the latest political stats.

"No, that can't be right." She sat the Styrofoam cup aside and sat upright in her swivel chair.

"What can't be right?" Fred Nunez paused at her desk carrying a handful of papers. He dropped several more pages on her desk before continuing toward his own desk. Collecting the morning's news bulletins for Elizabeth Sparks was not one of his duties, but it gave him the chance to see what was cooking in the real world before Elizabeth rewrote and changed things to suit her own taste. Besides, the news room was always in full-swing when she arrived, with other reporters trying to find interesting material for that evening's six o'clock broadcast. Management had more or less given her a free rein when it came to her sloppy work habits. Fred suspected it was due to her million-dollar smile and looks. She had already drawn the interest of several larger networks.

"These stats." Elizabeth held the printout high and tossed it on her cluttered desk.

"That's what I thought, but I double-checked and…" he nodded his head toward the papers, "they are pretty accurate. That's why I laid it on your desk. I know you and Curtis Roberts are pretty tight."

"Really? His rating jumped 15% over night? When's the last time that's happened?"

"Never."

"Well, then..." Elizabeth crossed the room to spread the printout on Fred's desk and leaned over his shoulder.

"What happened? Do you see anything I'm missing?"

"Nope." Fred took a sip of black coffee, and then looked over his shoulder to give her a grin.

"I didn't see anything on *that* piece of paper, but you did happen to show pictures of Curtis with Cynthia Quentero on last night's broadcast, didn't you?"

"Yeah, so? What's Cynthia Quentero got to do with Curtis' ratings taking that kind of a jump?"

Fred laughed loudly and shook his head.

"You're the investigative reporter. I'm just a cameraman. Why'd you have me shoot footage of him talking to Cindy if you didn't think it would help Curt's ratings"

"Because his speech was going nowhere. We were going to lose what audience we had." She heaved a deep sigh. So you think this jump had to do with her?

"That's all it could be, Liz—Curt being seen with Cynthia Quentero. She's a local girl who got shot saving several wounded soldiers under fire. Some of the men in her platoon say she deserves a Medal of Honor. She took over when their leader went down and she's responsible for saving the entire caravan. In short, she's a war hero, and the Central Valley likes heroes, especially female heroes."

Fred eased his chair around and held out his hand.

"I'll bet you the biggest steak dinner in town that I'm right. Deal?"

Elizabeth leaned over to kiss his cheek.

"No, make mine shrimp and I'll pay regardless of the outcome."

"Really? Why?"

"Because," Elizabeth said as she folded the printout, "I think you're right." She gave Fred a pat on the back.

"If anyone asks, I'm out of the office for a couple of hours chasing down a lead.

The Valley of Decision

******

Curtis paced the floor inside his campaign office located on the seedier side of McHenry Avenue, wedged between a used car lot and a tattoo parlor. It happened to be all his campaign budget would allow, something he never considered when he started this journey. At the moment he was caught in a heated discussion with his manager, Raymond Chandler, over sagging poll numbers. Neither of them had bothered to check that morning's results, since they had been consistently low from the beginning of the campaign. They both quieted and turned as Elizabeth Sparks entered. She paused in the middle of the room and took a quick glance around. The inside of the building was less appealing than the exterior.

She crossed the room without saying a word and took Curtis by the arm, then pulled him away from Raymond Chandler toward a vacant desk on the opposite wall. She unfolded the printouts and smoothed them with her palm.

"Take a look at these numbers. Your approval jumped 15% overnight, right after the interview with Robert and Cindy Quentero in front of the hospital."

Curtis leaned over the desk to study the polling numbers.

"Really? I haven't had a jump like that since ..."

"You've never had a jump like this, Curt," Elizabeth said, cutting him off. "In fact, you've been falling in the polls the past month. Even with the jump, you're trailing Walters by 12%. I'd advise doing another interview with them. Or, better yet, get some pictures of you and Cindy together."

"No, I don't like it," Raymond said loudly as he marched toward the desk.

"Why not?" Elizabeth said. "People love heroes, and she's a big one around here. Another interview with her and her brother would bring the numbers up even more, and some publicity pictures of him with Cindy, maybe holding her hand, would put them through the roof."

"Yes, but what about her feelings? She's a disabled veteran just back from the war and still healing. It would be using her tragedy and grief for personal gain. The answer is no!"

Raymond stormed toward the coffee machine and glanced over his shoulder as he filled his mug.

Elizabeth Sparks leaned close to Curt as she folded the printouts. She smelled of lilac and fresh soap. Her freshly painted lips brushed his ear as she talked in a whisper.

"Why do you listen to him? You're going to lose following his advice."

"He won the senate race for Patrick Adams. He's supposed to be very good at what he does," Curtis said close to her ear.

"Maybe," Elizabeth said, "but Patrick Adams was well known before he entered the race, and you're not. You need some publicity to pump life into your campaign, or you're going to die."

She folded the printouts and shoved them against his chest.

"You can't make a change if you don't get elected. That's the goal, isn't it? Think about it. I'd make a better campaign manager than he is."

She spun on her heel and walked briskly out the door. Curtis glanced at the folded papers in his hands then watched the door swing slowly shut as Elizabeth disappeared.

Chapter 4

"You have no idea how we felt, discovering you had been in Modesto for two weeks and not one phone call or a visit...nothing." Edith Fowler stood in Bobby Quentero's living room glaring at Cindy.

"Well, I've been meaning to call but..." Cindy shrugged.

"Well what? How hard is it to pick up a phone and dial our number? It's the same telephone number you grew up with. It hasn't changed one bit."

"I know, Ma. I know."

Cynthia tried hard to remember when she had started calling Edith Fowler mother, but any age or date of it happening escaped her. It had to be well after her own parents' deaths, and after her and Bobby had moved into the ranch house. Then, after a period of time, Mrs. Fowler became Mama.

"Well, if you knew, why didn't you call?"

"Because I was busy."

"Busy? Too busy to call me on the phone?"

"At first, yes. I wanted to visit Bobby and Karen and got to meet my niece and nephew. Then I had to make a doctor's appointment to see if Pete can't do something about my back. They wouldn't just let me walk in and see him, even if we're good friends. Then, I realized how much time had passed, and I was embarrassed to call. I'm really, really sorry, Mama. I really am."

"Well, good. You should be." Edith knelt beside Cindy's wheelchair and repeatedly kissed her cheeks as she wrapped her in a bear-hug.

"Oh, Lord, it's good to have you home. We've missed you so much."

"How's Seth?"

"Seth is doing just fine; he hasn't changed a bit. You'll get to see him and Miguel tonight."

"Oh? Are they coming over tonight?"

The crease between Edith's eyes grew more pronounced. "Cynthia Ann Quentero, are you trying to start an argument?"

"No, but you haven't asked me to move to the ranch or anything. It seems like you're assuming I just belong there."

"Well, you do belong there," Steven Fowler said in a booming voice. "So, where's your room, so we can start packing things?"

"Down the hall." Cindy pointed.

"I'll show you," Bobby said with a snicker.

"But we still have to talk about my moving back to the ranch." Cindy raised her voice. "I don't want to be a burden to anybody."

"Boy, you're gonna have fun with those two living under the same roof," Bobby said with a chuckle. "It'll seem like old times."

"Huh, I always thought they got along pretty good."

"Oh, they do," Bobby said as he opened Cindy's bedroom door. "Just like most mothers and daughters. Two head-strong women living together? Life in my patrol car will seem quieter."

******

Cindy stared out the window as the diesel engine in the new Ford pickup growled when Steven Fowler downshifted and turned west off the highway. She was amazed at how much of the landscape still looked familiar after two years. Steven accelerated to a comfortable sixty as Ray Price belted out *For the Good Times* on the CD player.

Peter shifted in the front passenger seat to grin at her. "Is it beginning to look familiar to you?"

"Yeah...some." She nodded. She waited a few seconds as the player began playing *Sunday Morning Coming Down.*

"When did you get the new truck," Cindy asked from the back seat.

Steven turned down the volume before answering.

"December 31, last year."

Edith reached over to pat Cindy on the arm. "He waited until an hour before closing time before telling that poor salesman we wanted the truck. He made him stay late on New Year's Eve," she said with a chuckle. "He believed he was going to get the best deal possible on last year's model."

"And I did too," Steven said.

"Yes, maybe you did. But you didn't have to make the salesman work late. He had a wife and two small children waiting on him. I'm sure they wanted him home."

"You say that, but we don't really know. That picture on his desk could be of anybody. He might've put it there just to sell cars."

Peter burst out laughing. "I haven't heard this one before."

"Steven Fowler," Edith said giggling. "Do you really believe that?"

"No, but it got a rise out of you," he said as he slowed to turn through the gate into the Fowler cattle ranch.

Cindy craned her neck to see the high metal gate posts forming an arch that supported a large letter "F" with wings. The sight made her feel warm inside. The truck slowed to a crawl as a black and white border collie trotted off the front porch of a rambling ranch house to bark a greeting at the truck.

"Jasper!" Cindy said over the lump in her throat. "My Lord, how I've missed that dog."

"Yeah, I bet you did," Peter said. "You two were inseparable; you even let him sleep on your bed."

"He was lonely." She opened the door and Jasper paused to study her and sniff her leg before jumping into the truck to give her several wet licks.

"Hi Jasper. How's my best friend ever?" She kissed him on the snout.

"We had to retire him to the house and barn area," Edith said as she got out of the truck.

"He's still got the heart, but his old legs won't keep up with the other dogs. He tries, but it's really hard on him," Peter said as he reached into the truck bed and retrieved her wheelchair. He grinned at Cindy and the dog before giving a sharp whistle.

"Jasper, here! You've got to move so Cindy can get out." The dog jumped out of the truck and barked several times. Cynthia slipped one arm around Peter's neck as he lifted her from the truck and into the wheelchair.

"I never thought much about it when I signed up, but I really missed this place." She rolled the chair forward then stopped to stare at the ramp.

"Wow! You did a lot of work," Cindy said.

"That's what I was trying to say back in my office," Peter said.

"How long has it been here?"

"Several weeks before you were released from the V.A. hospital."

"I guess no one listened to a word I said about not moving back in, did they?"

"Oh, we listened, dear," Edith said as she grabbed the handles on the wheelchair and rolled the chair up the ramp. "But we figured we might need the ramp regardless if you moved in or not. That way you could come for visits, if nothing else." Edith held the door open.

"Welcome to your new home. I want you to treat this house as your own, because that is exactly what it is. And we're your family. Now, come. Let's get your room set up.

The men will get your dresser and clothes from Bobby's, but you may want to move things around some."

"I have to see Doctor Hastings tomorrow morning," Cindy said.

"I'll take you," Edith said as she propped the door open. "It's almost lunch time. I'll fix something to eat, once we decide on your room. What do you feel like eating?"

******

The men watched as the screen door slammed shut and Edith's voice floated toward them.

"Well," Steven said with a laugh. "I reckon your ma's happy. She's got another project and someone to take care of." He opened the driver's door to the truck and motioned with his head.

"Hop in, if you've got a minute. Let's go check on the cattle. They're probably ready to move to the fall pasture."

******

Cindy paused to stare into the bedroom while Edith opened and closed a closet door. It was the same bedroom she had used for twelve years after her parents deaths, except the doorway had been widened to accommodate her wheelchair. Outside of a fresh coat of pale blue paint and a new throw-rug, the room remained the same. Someone had taken pains to rehang the pictures where they had been. The picture of her racing Kiowa Dawn around a barrel at the Turlock rodeo hung above the bed. The picture of her and Kiowa Dawn standing beside her blue pickup hung in the hallway opposite the bedroom door. The photo gave her pause. She hadn't seen either of them in two years. She loved that truck and had scraped, saved and worked her fingers to the bone to buy it. Becky had told her it had been stored inside the barn and covered with a tarp the day she left for

Afghanistan.

She inched farther into the room. Several photos of her with Bobby, Peter and Becky took up the remaining wall inside the room.

"I hope there's enough room to hang your clothes," Edith said.

"I'm positive there's more than enough room, Mom. My wardrobe is pretty limited nowadays."

"Oh, I'm sorry. I didn't think..." Edith stammered. "Do you mind me asking if everything else is okay with the room?"

"Everything's great Mom. And as far as the clothes go, I've got plenty of dresses and things at Bobby's house. It's just trying to put them on when my legs don't work. That's why I mostly wear these," she said pulling on her Marine T-shirt.

"Oh," Edith said with a smile. "Then maybe I can help you get all fancied up sometime and we'll go out to dinner."

"I don't want to be any trouble. You've got enough on your plate with me just being here and having to take me to my doctor appointments."

"Na, it's no trouble at all...really," she added when Cindy frowned. "It's going to be fun just having you here. Besides, I'll be the pest. You'll have to tell me to back off once in a while."

Cindy guided her wheelchair to the head of the bed and picked up a small framed photograph from the night stand. It was of two small children laughing as the boy pushed a girl in a swing.

"You were what..., about five or six when that was taken," Edith said.

"Yeah, we were celebrating Pete's birthday at the park. We ate hotdogs and chips, and you had a chocolate cake with ice cream." Cindy chuckled and shook her head. "I think he spent more time pushing me in the swing than celebrating his sixth birthday." She placed the picture back on the night stand.

"I can't believe you still have it."

"It hasn't moved since Bobby bought his house in Modesto and you joined the Marines. As far as I'm concerned, it'll stay that way," Edith said.

Chapter 5

Cindy didn't know which she hated more, the hospital gown that opened down the back or the fact that one of the doctors she was seeing was a man she had known her entire life. Growing up together, she had shared peanut butter and grape jelly sandwiches with Peter Fowler, played football with him and fished in the pond. They had done most everything together. But allowing him to see her naked body was one of the few things they had not done, and he'd never tried.

"He's a doctor, Cindy," Becky said with a giggle. "He sees dozens of women every day. At least you get to keep your underwear on. Feel grateful he's not giving you a breast exam or he'd be...."

"I know, Becky, I had a couple of them in the Marines. It's just that..."

"It's just that it's Pete looking at your backside, isn't it?" Becky laughed as Cindy flushed and looked away. "It is. Look at you. I think that's the first time I've seen you blush. I'll make sure to keep your butt covered," she said as the door opened.

Peter was standing at the foot of the examination table with a middle-aged man sporting a short beard and a warm smile.

"Cindy, this is Doctor Randy Hastings. I've shown him your file and he's asked to see you."

Cindy shook Dr. Hastings' hand and smiled. "Randy Hastings. How come that name sounds familiar?

"Maybe because I'm Edith Fowler's primary

physician. But I also know something about spinal injuries. That's why I'm here today. I understand you and Doctor Fowler go way back. Is that true?"

"Yeah, we've known each other since I was five."

"That's what he was saying," Doctor Hastings said, glancing over Cindy's chart one more time.

"How's my back look, Doc? Is it a big mess?"

"Actually, it's not as bad as you'd think."

"Really?"

"Yes, really. Don't get me wrong, the bullet did some pretty extensive damage, but it's not as bad as I was expecting. Let me put it this way—

I've seen a lot worse."

He took her right foot and began flexing her ankle and knee as he talked. "I'm not going to make any promises, but we might be able to get you back on your feet with a walker."

"That would be great," Cindy said. "A whole lot better than being stuck in that thing." She pointed toward the wheelchair.

"Yes, but you'd be a lot worse off without it. Let's get started, shall we? Please lie on your back." Dr. Hastings helped her to lie back on the table. He began pushing on her stomach.

"How does that feel? Do you feel anything at all?"

"It feels like you're trying to squash me. I can feel the pressure, but nothing else."

Dr. Hastings glanced at Becky.

"Help her to lie on her stomach."

Becky took extra care in making sure the split in the robe didn't reveal too much as she rolled Cindy to her stomach. She chuckled and leaned close to Cindy's ear.

"You didn't have to worry, because Pete turned his back while you rolled over." She finished by covering Cindy's bottom with a towel.

Dr. Hastings began pressing on her lower back.

"How does that feel? Anything?"

"About the same. Pressure, but that's all."

"That's good," Dr. Hastings said with a nod. "You're not in any pain. Roll over. I want to check your legs."

Becky helped Cindy as she struggled to her back.

"You have good muscle tone," he said flexing her legs."

"We did a lot of running in the Marines."

"Yes, but according to your chart, that's been over a year ago. You can lose a lot in that amount of time."

"Oh, that's because either Pete or Becky come by every night and make me lay on the floor while they stretch me like a rubber band."

"That's good. Whatever they're doing seems to be working." He helped Cindy into a sitting position. "What Pete should have done was to talk you out of joining the Marines and running off to Afghanistan and getting shot in the first place. You should have been home raising babies."

"Now, that makes you a little old fashioned and chauvinistic, doesn't it?" Cindy said with a snort.

"Maybe, but it seldom cripples or kills women."

She laughed and shook her head. "Pete couldn't have stopped me. We're only friends, not married. He's only kissed me once, in fun."

"That's not what he told me. He told me he's crazy about you."

"Really?" Cindy cocked her head and laughed.

"What I actually said was, you drive me crazy," Peter said flexing her left foot and ankle much like what Dr. Hastings had done moments earlier with her right leg. "I think someone will need to put a leash on you when we get you back on your feet."

He pulled a retracted ballpoint pen from his shirt pocket and ran it across the bottom of her left foot and received a slight jerk. Peter pulled back with a surprised look.

"You felt that?"

Cindy leaned forward, trying to see her feet. "I don't

know. I think I felt something."

He repeated the action and got the same result, then turned toward Dr. Hastings. "Did you see that?"

"Yes, I did. Try the other foot."

Pete repeated the action on her right foot.

"Hmm, not as much, but definitely something."

"What's it mean?" Cindy asked.

"It could mean nothing. I'd like to run some tests." Dr. Hastings began typing on the computer as he talked.

"Becky? After you help her get dressed, I'd like you to order an M. R. I., complete blood work, and a CT scan."

"Yes, Doctor."

Doctor Hastings turned to Cynthia.

"You'll be getting calls from the different departments telling you when to come in, so make sure to have someone lined up to bring you."

"Can't you get those things from the V. A.?"

"Maybe, but something changed. I want to know what's going on right now. Doctor Fowler will call you when we get the results." He stood and shook Cindy's hand with a warm smile. "It was nice finally meeting you. You're about all I've heard about since this guy's known you were coming back to Modesto."

"You're joking." Cindy looked at Peter, who turned his back on her while pretending to inventory the cabinet.

Dr. Hastings paused with his hand on the door knob.

"Oh, what's this I hear about a veteran's center you're planning?"

"Where'd you hear that?"

"From Peter." Dr. Hastings said. "You told his mom, she told him, and he told me. It helps to have connections."

"It's only a dream at this point. I don't have any money or anything on paper.

"Well, count me in when you do get it going. I'll donate some time every now and then."

"You can count on me also, and my lunk of a brother too," Becky said.

I've got to run," Dr. Hastings said, checking his watch. "I'll see you again when we get the test results."

Chapter 6

Fred Nunez glanced up from reading today's schedule as Elizabeth Sparks entered the news room fifteen minutes late, carrying a stack of papers in her right hand and a Starbucks latte in the other. He returned to reading the schedule, trying to will her away. Having Elizabeth around usually meant trouble or more work, no matter how you sliced it. He was beginning to think she had left when the stack of paper she was carrying dropped on his desk.

"I want to know everything about this woman," she said, leaning across his desk.

Fred glanced at the stack and snorted. A photograph of Cynthia Quentero he had taken himself the day she returned home stared back at him.

"That's easy," Fred took a sip from his coffee mug to find it empty. "She's a multi-decorated veteran, including the Silver Star, for saving a convoy and pulling two wounded soldiers to safety under fire." He leaned back in his chair and pointed toward a door.

"They've got an entire Bible on Cynthia Quentero in the vault. Help yourself."

"I would, but I don't know where to look, and Stanley has me stuck on the teacher's strike," she whined, as she batted her blue eyes at him.

"Please," she pleaded as Fred stared silently. "I'm going to need your help on this one.

"I'm a cameraman, Liz, not your gopher," Fred said after a few more minutes of silent staring.

"I know, Fred, but this will be good for both of us.

Do you like doing teacher's strikes and Christians protesting Planned Parenthood?"

Fred was still glaring, so Elizabeth heaved a sigh. "Come on, Fred. Pleeese."

"What's in it for me, Liz? Hanging around you usually gets me in trouble with Stanley, while you boogie off without a simple *thank you.*"

She gritted her teeth and pulled two tickets from her purse.

"Would a couple of Giants tickets to Saturday's game against the Astros help change your mind?"

Fred snatched the tickets from her hand and the stack of paper she had dropped on his desk.

"I'll have a photocopy of everything I can lay my hands on this afternoon. What kind of stuff are you looking for? Skeletons in the closet?"

"No, just the opposite," Elizabeth said. "I want to know who she is, what she likes and what she doesn't like. I want to know what she eats and does she have any lovers?"

Fred laughed and leaned back in his chair, tapping the tickets against the desk.

"Don't take too long, Fred," she said. "I've got a feeling Stan's going to want us to film the picket line. He's already asked me to come up with a bunch of questions to ask the teachers."

"Well, you won't get any of the stuff you're wanting in the vault," Fred said with a grin. "What you'll get is the same garbage they put in newspapers. You want to know Lieutenant Quentero? I've known her as long as the Fowlers. Grab a pen and some paper and I'll tell you about her. Bobby and Cindy both lived at the Fowler ranch after their parents got killed in an automobile accident. Bobby was in junior high, and Cindy was in 5th or 6th grade at the time."

Elizabeth grinned as she grabbed a pen and pad from Fred's desk.

"First and foremost, she's a dyed-in-the-wool Christian. So is her brother. In fact, they all are—Cindy and the Fowlers."

Fred poured two cups of coffee and handed one to Elizabeth.

"Bobby Quentero used to carry one of those Gideon New Testaments around, but not Cindy. She carried the entire Bible in her purse, and held Bible studies in a corner of the lunchroom. Some of us guys used to make fun of her, but she never paid us any mind."

Fred took a sip of coffee and leaned back in his chair grinning.

"She's quite the woman, even back then. She loves sports, and could out-bat, out-catch, and run faster than half the baseball team."

"This is great," Elizabeth said, nodding her head. "Did she have any boyfriends?"

Fred shook his head laughing.

"Not Cindy. A few guys tried, but never got anywhere. Eddy tried getting cute one day, and slapped her on the butt. In turn, Cindy slapped him senseless. When Bobby heard about it, he cleaned Eddy's clock in the gym. Then Pete finished the job in the school parking lot a day later. We stayed clear of her after that. Besides, looking back at it, I think she had some plans to become a missionary or a woman pastor.

"She's a real carnivore. She'll eat any kind of meat—hamburgers, steaks, bacon or sausage. Nothing's off her menu. And the thing is, she stays thin as a rail."

"Yeah, she's the kind the rest of us women love to hate," Elizabeth said with a snort. She flipped the page and glanced at Fred.

"Keep going. This stuff's golden."

"She's crazy about vanilla ice cream cones dipped in chocolate."

Chapter 7

Cindy was seated in her wheelchair on the front lawn scratching Jasper behind the ears when Peter came through the door carrying two mugs of coffee. He handed one to Cindy and sat next to her in a lawn chair.

"Thanks, "she said, taking a sip. "Whoa, that's hot."

"Right out of the pot," Peter said with a smile.

"So, do you actually think you and Doctor Hastings will ever get me back on my feet?"

Peter took a thoughtful sip of coffee and nodded. I don't want to make any promises, but sure, there's always a chance. It'll be a lot of work and it won't be easy.

Jasper broke away from Cindy and raced toward the gate barking as a dark blue Cadillac Escalade pulled into the yard and rolled to a stop in the driveway. The driver's door opened and Curtis climbed out, followed by Elizabeth Sparks, who exited the passenger side, checking a new camera that was slung around her neck.

"Huh," Cindy said as Curtis came closer. "Hello Curt, what brings you way out here?"

"Actually, I came to see you." He flashed Cindy his best vote-winning smile.

"That's nice," she said as Elizabeth approached. "Aren't you going to introduce us to your girlfriend?"

"Who, Liz? She's not my girlfriend."

Elizabeth brushed past Curtis and extended her right hand to Cindy.

"Hi, I'm Elizabeth Sparks, and I'm helping Curt's campaign, which is being run almost as badly as his manners."

"Yes," Cindy said as she took the hand. "We met in front of the hospital. I just like getting under Curt's skin."

"Good. He needs a woman to keep him in line because he hasn't a clue of what's involved in trying to get elected."

Cindy turned toward Curtis. "I like her. She's got you pegged pretty good."

Peter cleared his throat as he stood.

"I've got to get back to the hospital. Can I get either of you a cup of coffee before I leave?"

"Nope," Curtis said, shaking his head. "I passed my limit around ten this morning.

Elizabeth smiled as she laid a warm hand against Peter's arm. "No, but thank you."

Peter leaned over to give Cindy a quick hug.

"I'll be on call most of the night, but Becky will check on you later."

Cindy watched as he walked toward his car before yelling, "See you Thursday afternoon."

Peter waved then started his car and drove away. Curtis waited a few seconds before pulling the lawn chair next to Cindy and smiled as he sat next to her.

"So, how do you like living on a cattle ranch?"

The sound of a digital camera caused them both to look at Elizabeth. She had her camera pointed toward them.

"That's a great picture," she said, looking at the screen on the back of the camera. She brought the camera to Cindy and showed her the picture.

"Yes, it is a nice picture," Cindy said, nodding. It really was a nice picture, she thought. The color and focus was perfect. The only thing she didn't like about the picture was that Curtis' plastered grin made it look like a political ad.

"Do you mind if I take another? Elizabeth asked.

"Me?" Cindy said.

"You don't mind, do you?

"No, I don't mind."

"Great."

Elizabeth smiled and motioned with her hand to stage

the next shot, moving Curt closer to Cindy.

"That's good, Curt. Now, take Cindy's hand and smile at her."

The camera clicked several times.

"Yes, just one more."

Elizabeth shifted her own position as the camera clicked again.

"Oh yes," Elizabeth bubbled, "you're going to love this one. Okay, okay," she said, repositioning Curtis. "Just one more."

She moved toward them and motioned with her hands.

"Curt, mover closer. Closer; I want your face next to hers."

Curtis leaned over to place his head next to Cynthia's.

"That's it. Great! Now, smile."

******

Peter was sitting with his mother and father in his parents' living room, watching the evening news on TV. An attractive brunette was talking in front of a backdrop of police cars and rescue vehicles with flashing lights at the scene of a multi-car pile-up on Highway 99. The caption at the bottom of the screen identified her as news anchor, Rita Lorenzo. The screen changed and Elizabeth Sparks suddenly appeared behind Rita. Steven hit the volume control as Rita shifted her chair to look at Elizabeth's image.

"Now, on a lighter note, let's join Elizabeth Sparks on the campaign trail with Curtis Roberts. We understand the race has tightened. Is that correct?"

"That's right, Rita," Elizabeth said, flashing a million-dollar smile at the camera. "The poles have tightened, and Curtis' approval numbers have taken another 8% jump."

"So, what caused this move in the polls? Can we attribute it to the interview with Lieutenant Quentero and her family in front of the hospital?" Rita said, flashing a smile of her own.

"I'm sure that had some influence on the numbers, but a number of people I talked to say they are deeply concerned with the increase in crime in our area."

The television screen suddenly changed to Elizabeth at the Vintage Fair Shopping Mall holding a microphone in front of a man who was shaking his head.

"Yeah, that's something that has to be taken care of. It ain't safe for a man's wife and kids inside their home anymore."

The screen suddenly changed again to show her with the microphone in front of a middle-aged woman. The woman sniffed as she dabbed at her eyes with a tissue.

"What happened to that poor woman broke my heart. Imagine, someone driving by your house shooting. She lost her little girl who was sleeping in her own bed. I send my prayers out to them."

"I can't argue with her on that subject," Edith said with a tinge of anger in her voice. "God must have a special place in hell for someone who'd shoot a baby sleeping in their crib.

Peter glanced at his mother and gave a slight nod.

A close-up of Elizabeth's face appeared on the TV. "But the real surprise came when Curtis decided to leave the campaign trail yesterday and visit Miss Quentero at the Fowler family ranch."

The screen on the television suddenly changed to show a photograph of Curtis sitting in their lawn chair and holding Cynthia's hand. Peter set his cup of coffee on the coffee table and snickered.

"Liz must have taken those after I left. Too bad Cindy's sleeping. She'd like to see these."

"That's my favorite lawn chair," Steven growled. "I'll have to fumigate it now."

The picture on the television changed again to show Curtis holding Cindy's hand and smiling at the camera. It quickly switched again to show his head next to hers and smiling.

"That *is* a different move for Candidate Roberts to

make," Rita said. "He's usually so serious about running for election. What can you tell us about his visit? Did he ask any questions about her being wounded in the war, or her medals?"

"No," Elizabeth said with a bubbly tone. "This was simply one friend visiting another and catching up on old times. What most people don't know is, Curtis Roberts and Cynthia Quentero attended the same high school, and were close friends. There was no mention of the war or that terrible night she was wounded. Curtis was seeing his old classmate."

Steven laughed loudly and swatted Peter on the shoulder. "Hey, you should've stuck around some. She might've taken your picture too. We coulda been looking at you on TV."

Peter shook his head and laughed. "No, I think Elizabeth would've edited me out, Pop. I'm not big news like Cindy. Curt wants to be seen with her, not me."

"Why not," Edith said. "You're a good doctor."

"Me and a thousand other doctors around here, Mom. That's not news. But Cindy joining the Marines and going off to war and coming home wounded … now that's news. That's why Elizabeth took all those pictures."

"Liz took the pictures herself?" Edith said.

"Yeah, she had the camera, and I don't see any of her," Peter said.

"Hmm," Edith said, sipping her coffee. "She's a better photographer than a reporter. She ought to stick with it."

Steven Fowler got up and headed toward the kitchen.

"Don't let her hear you say that. She thinks she's the next best thing to popcorn. I'm going to get some more coffee. Anyone else care for some?"

Chapter 8

Cindy dropped her arms to her sides and let the dumbbells roll from her hands. She lay on the floor glaring at her brother who stood straddled over her feet. Peter had been called to the hospital for an emergency, and Becky had gone on a day trip to Yosemite with some friends. Robert happened to be visiting and happily volunteered to help her with her daily exercises. She had accepted, thinking how sweet it was of her brother wanting to help her. That admiration soon turned to angry glares and snipes. Her sweat-soaked T-shirt clung to her exhausted body as she gasped for air.

"Come on," Robert urged, "come on. Twenty more."

"Go jump in the cow pond. "I'm tired. Give me a break."

"I didn't think Marines ever gave up. Isn't that always what you used to tell me? Give me twenty more reps."

"I'm serious, Bobby. I quit. Besides, what do you know about Marines? You never belonged to the corps."

"No, but I'm a cop," Robert said. "We go through basic training too. So, come on. You're a Quentero, and Quenteros don't give up. Ever!"

He grabbed her right arm and shoved the dumbbell into her palm and started moving it.

"Aghhh!" Cindy growled as she swung her left arm, almost clubbing Robert with the other dumbbell.

"That's it!" Robert yelled. "Come on, that's it! See, you've still got a lot left in you."

Cindy gritted her teeth and started doing another set of arm lifts.

"What...difference...does it make?" she said between lifts. "I still can't walk."

"The doc said there was a good chance you will, so keep going."

She dropped the weights to her sides, gasping for air.

"There, that's another twenty. And Doctor Hastings said there was a *chance* I might walk someday. He didn't say there was a *good chance*."

"Yeah, but Pete said ...."

"What's Peter know?" Cindy said, cutting him off. "He's a horse doctor."

Robert straddled her with his hands on his hips and glared down at her.

"So, you wanna give up and be stuck in that chair all your life, getting fat and ugly, having people wait on you hand and foot, and feeling sorry for yourself?"

Cindy released a loud "Aaahhh" as she grabbed both of his legs with her arms, causing him to fall beside her. Quickly grabbing one of Robert's arms, she twisted it, pinning it to his back.

"Ow! Hey, wait!" Robert yelled.

"What's the matter, can't stand having your little sister kick your butt?"

"No, no, wait. Take a look at your leg!"

Craning her neck, Cindy gasped at the sight of her left leg slung across Robert's waist, pinning him to the carpet.

"How'd you do that?" Robert was saying.

"I – I don't know."

Robert jumped to his feet, digging his cell phone from his pocket. He started punching numbers. "Pete's gotta hear 'bout this, even if you think he's a horse doctor."

******

Becky Fowler and Edith helped Cindy with her examination robe then waited for Pete who was with another patient. It had taken a day to squeeze her in between appointments, and Cindy had spent a good portion of the evening hours trying to make her legs work with no results. Now, she sat on the examination table staring at her useless legs as Edith and Becky gossiped and laughed. She felt beads of sweat on her brow as she tried to will her limbs to work, but got nothing for the effort.

She took a deep breath and released it slowly, staring at the photographs on the wall. Several were of different horses from the ranch, then a close-up of Jasper with his tongue hanging out. Finally, there was one of Peter pushing her in a swing when they were teenagers. The door finally opened and Peter entered, reading her chart.

"Bobby said you got angry because he was pushing you to do your exercises?"

"Well, I'd done everything that you and Becky make me do but, well you know how he is. He was acting like my drill sergeant, trying to get more out of me. I was tired." She glanced once more at her legs hanging over the edge of the examination table.

Peter laughed as he slipped a pair of blue latex gloves on his hands. "Well, for whatever reason, it seemed to work, didn't it? He got a lot more out of you than Becky and I do. Let's see what you can do without Bobby. Try moving your left leg."

Cindy tensed her upper body and gritted her teeth, but nothing happened.

"That's okay," Peter said. "Take a breath and try again."

She tried twice more with the same result. She finally broke down with a cry of frustration and beat against both legs with her fists as several tears spilled over.

"Work, stupid legs. Why won't you work?

Peter slipped both arms around her and held her against his chest, caressing her hair with his palm.

"It's okay, it's okay. We know you *can* move them, and that's enough for now. We'll try again later."

"But why can't I move them now?"

Peter grinned as he sat on the rolling stool and typed something into the computer.

"My guess is you were angry with your brother and weren't thinking about your legs. That's how you could move them. It was automatic."

"Maybe we should get Bobby over here next time she comes," Becky said. "He could pester her some more."

"Not a bad idea," Edith said. "If he'd pester her like he did when they were teenagers, he'd have her chasing him down the hall."

Cindy chuckled as Edith handed her a tissue.

"Thanks, you guys."

Peter gave her another hug, and she leaned back to pat him on the chest.

"I got your shirt all wet with tears."

"That's okay, I've got more in the closet," he said.

He kissed her on the top of her head and smiled.

"We'll try again later."

Chapter 9

"Just like we did before," Peter said as he slipped his arm beneath Cynthia's knees.

"What are we doing?" she said, slipping both arms around his neck.

"There's no use in you staying cooped-up inside this old house all the time." Peter lifted her out of the wheelchair and placed her into the front passenger seat in his pickup.

"May I ask where you're taking me?"

"Just a little tour of the ranch. You haven't really seen anything but the house and front yard since you've been home, have you?"

"No," she said shaking her head. "Has it changed much?"

"No, just the opposite," Peter said with a laugh. He started the truck and turned onto the field road that circled the ranch. "It's a perfect museum of a turn-of-the-century cattle ranch. Outside of a little fresh paint once in a while, and replacing something that's broken or worn out, it hasn't changed a lot since my great grandpa bought it a hundred and twenty years ago."

"Let's do it," she said with a grin. Cindy allowed her eyes to roam across the cattle-covered pasture they were passing. It was the same one where Peter used to let her win when they raced their horses. In fact, she thought, it was Peter who taught her how to ride a horse properly.

"That's something you haven't seen," Peter said, pointing toward a fairly new well near a large watering trough. "That's Seth's idea from start to finish. It got pretty dry during the drought last year, and cattle take a lot of water. It has an electronic switch that'll turn on the pump automatically and shut it off."

"That'll make things a little easier," she said with a nod. "He'll make a good rancher someday."

"Dad says he's a natural-born cattleman in the making."

Cindy's eyes were feeling heavy by the time Peter turned the truck and headed slowly back toward the ranch house. She couldn't have told him half of what they discussed, but it was good just being with Peter. He made her feel comfortable, like an old shirt or blanket. No, she decided, it was more than that. She couldn't picture life without having Peter around. *Too bad*, she thought, *he was her brother.*

******

Zoe Shultz sat alone in the city park beneath an ancient oak tree with her knees drawn up against her chest. Her mother and Carl Mongrove were having another fight and Zoe had discovered the hard way the safest place to be while they were fighting was anywhere else. She had been the recipient of a flying ashtray and had to have three stitches above her right eye. A little lower and she might have lost an eye. She had no idea what caused this fight, and didn't particularly care.

On top of the picnic table under the neighboring tree a young girl dressed in a short skirt was busy giving a boy a lesson on dental hygiene with their lips locked.

Zoe had had a special boyfriend once. He was older and drove a nice car. He smelled good also. They dated about six months. Then she told him she was pregnant and she never saw him again. After that, there were several guys she liked, but they only wanted the same thing. That's when she discovered it was easier to look different and not let anyone close. But it didn't stop the loneliness. She believed she was born with a great big hole in the center of her chest that ached constantly, and it grew worse whenever she saw a display of passion, such as the one currently happening at the picnic bench.

Zoe shifted to the opposite side of the tree so she would not have to see the hygiene lesson. *Give me a break,* she whispered as a man and a woman standing beside a parked car wrapped their arms around each other and kissed.

She sniffed and buried her face against her knees as the pain in her chest grew worse.

Oh God, make it go away. Please God.

There were times she thought she would die.

I just want someone to love and take care of me.

Chapter 10

The sun was warm and pleasant, causing Steven Fowler to stretch and yawn. Edith was sitting on the porch beside him shelling green peas while they watched Peter and Cynthia toss a football. Steven leaned back in his chair placing his dusty boots on the railing and sipped his iced tea. Jasper barked and ran, chasing the football.

"Does it seem like Pete's been spending more time at the ranch lately," Steven said.

Edith smiled warmly as she shelled another pod. "Yes, it does. Do you have a problem with that?"

"No, not at all. But we used to feel lucky if he dropped by once every week or so. Now, he's here every other day."

"I have a feeling Cindy might have something to do with that," Edith said.

"I think you might be right," Steven said with a laugh.

When the telephone rang, Edith set the bowl of peas on the porch and scampered inside. Steve cocked his head in an effort to catch her voice inside the kitchen.

"Hello? No, this is Edith Fowler. Yes, she's here. May I ask whose calling? Okay, I'll ask her."

Edith came back out to the porch with her hand covering the receiver.

"Cindy? It's Curtis Roberts. He wants to talk to you. Are you up to taking any calls?"

Cindy looked toward Peter, and then toward Steven before nodding.

"Yeah, sure; why not?"

She rolled her chair toward the porch and reached for

the phone. "What's he want?"

"I don't know, honey. You'll have to ask him."

Cynthia took the receiver and slowly raised it to her ear, while studying the faces of Peter and his father, as if expecting one of them to say something. "Hello?"

******

"Cindy? Yeah, hi. How are you doing?"

Curtis leaned back in a swivel chair inside his campaign office with a cup of coffee and his feet propped on the desk.

"I'm doing okay. Why do you ask?"

"I heard through the grapevine that you were able to move your legs a little, and wanted to say I think that's great."

"How did you hear about that?'

Curtis laughed. "I'm a politician, and I've got my sources. So, I thought I'd call and say congratulations."

"Really, that's sweet of you, but it was only one leg and I haven't been able to do it since." Cindy gave a crooked grin as she shrugged her shoulders and looked at Peter.

"But you're talking to an old beat-up soldier," Cindy added. "I'll win this battle sooner or later. I can handle it."

Curtis took a sip of coffee, and then placed the cup on the desk as he sat upright, letting his feet hit the floor with a thud.

"Maybe you are," he said. "But yeah, I think you can win the battle. But if things get tough, give me a call. Even old soldiers hurt and sometimes need a shoulder to cry on."

"Yeah," Cindy said quietly. "I guess we do. Thanks."

"Hey, I've got this thing I've got to go to Friday night. They want me to give a little speech. It's a small fundraiser, to be honest. I was wondering if you'd like to go with me."

Cindy laughed. "Are you asking me on a date?"

"No...well I guess you could call it that, except I'll be working. But I know the people would love to meet you. You might even say a few words, if you don't mind."

"Oh, I don't think so, Curtis," Cindy shook her head.

"I've never done anything like that before. I wouldn't know what to say."

"That's the great thing about it, Cindy. You wouldn't have to prepare a thing. Just tell them a little about yourself, and maybe mention what your plans are. It would mean a lot to the people, and it would help me out."

Cindy listened to his breathing for several seconds as she rubbed her eyes with the fingers of her right hand as though they were tired.

"Please, Cindy. Besides, I hear you're thinking of starting some sort of rehabilitation center. You could mention something about that. It might be a way to gain support for your project. The people who will be there love to give money to a good cause. How about it? It would mean a lot to me."

"Boy," Cindy said with a chuckle, "you do have your sources. It's like talking to the C.I.A. Yeah, sure. Can you pick me up?"

"Great. I'll pick you up at the ranch around 5:30. Wear your uniform. That would be a nice touch."

"If it fits. I've gained a few pounds."

"Maybe you can get Mrs. Fowler to let it out for you if it doesn't fit. Well look, I've got to run. I'll pick you up on Friday. Bye."

"Goodbye." Cindy handed the phone to Edith.

Curtis hung up the phone then grinned as he pumped his fist in the air. "Yes!"

Chapter 11

Curtis' small crowd gathering happened to be inside a large hotel banquet room packed with people. Curtis insisted that she would be on stage with him as he gave his speech. She balked at the idea, saying just being there was quite enough.

"Yeah, yeah, I know it was huge for you to even come, and I really, really appreciate it, Cindy. I really do." Curtis stared at her with his baby-blue eyes. "But I really need you there. Believe me, I sometimes get nervous when I'm giving a speech, but I'm not that way when you're with me."

"Now, that's gigantic whopper if I've ever heard one."

"No, I'm telling the truth," Curtis pouted.

"Oh, okay," Cindy said as she pointed her chair toward the handicap ramp to the stage. "If what you said is true, you need to leave politics alone and find another profession."

That was almost an hour ago. She said a silent prayer, asking God to make the speech end soon so she could go to the lady's room. Plus, she was certain she wasn't the only woman in the room who felt the same. But Curtis went on without a hint of break.

She glanced toward the gray-headed gentleman seated next to her who had only spoken a few words all night, but had a winning smile. She guessed maybe he had given a large donation to Curtis' campaign otherwise, what was he doing on stage? She returned her attention toward Curtis' back. He was beginning to sound as if he might be winding down his campaign speech.

"Just like most of you seated in this room, I have become increasingly tired of seeing our over-worked police and firemen being asked to do an impossible task, and for less money."

He paused as the audience broke into applause.

"I won't stand before you and make empty promises that I don't intend to keep…like my opponent."

He took a sip of water as the audience broke into another round of applause.

"But I will promise to do everything I can to turn as much power and tax dollars possible back to our local community here in Modesto, California."

Cynthia caught a glimpse of Elizabeth Sparks as she rose and made her way toward the door.

Probably going to the potty, lucky woman. She glared at Elizabeth's back. *Ahhh, I hate you! You might have to mop up the stage if Curt doesn't hurry.*

She changed her mind as Elizabeth smiled and paused at several tables on the way toward the door. Then, she stopped just inside the door to applaud with the audience. Curtis wiped his brow and removed the microphone from the stand. He stepped away from the podium as he cleared his throat.

"Now, since we have charged everyone in the room $250.00 a plate for dinner, I guess I should make it up to you by introducing the pretty lady seated behind me." He gestured grandly with a sweep of his arm.

"Ladies and gentlemen, I would like you to meet my personal and almost life-long friend, Lieutenant Cynthia Quentero." He handed Cynthia the microphone as everyone rose in a standing ovation.

The urge to use the restroom suddenly left as she stared at the crowd. She cleared her throat twice before speaking.

"My. I don't know what to say after that welcome. I guess I should start by scolding Curtis for not telling me the truth. He told me this was a small and informal gathering. I was under the impression we were going to meet some people at a backyard barbecue."

The audience broke into laughter as Curtis leaned his head next to hers in order to talk into the microphone. A dozen or more flashes from cameras erupted as he spoke.

"Sorry folks. I had to tell her that fib to get her here, or she would still be at the Fowler cattle ranch."

"Maybe," Cindy said with a crooked grin. "But I will certainly ask specific questions before agreeing to attend anymore fundraisers."

Curtis pulled a chair close to sit next to her.

She stared at him for a few seconds before turning back to the crowd. "I honestly don't know what to say. Curtis asked me to say a little about myself, but I'm sure most of you already know who I am, and that I was wounded in Afghanistan. We lost three men that evening, so I am reluctant to talk about myself."

Curtis leaned close to her again. "If you don't wish to talk about yourself, then why don't you tell us about the rehabilitation center you are planning?"

"Oh, it's simply an idea I had. We don't have anything on paper," she said, shaking her head.

"That's okay. Go ahead and tell us about your idea."

Cynthia smiled weakly as several more cameras flashed.

"Well," she spoke softly into the microphone. "We've all heard of what some are calling the "V. A. scandal, and the lack of treatment for many veterans. Most of the V. A. doctors are hard-working, underpaid, and handicapped with regulations and paperwork."

She rolled her chair to the edge of the stage. "Approximately twenty-two veterans commit suicide daily, and that needs to stop. I envision a center privately run, and small enough to treat each veteran personally, perhaps run by a volunteer staff. I have already talked to two local physicians and one registered nurse who said they are willing to donate time, and promised to find other doctors who will help. We want to treat the entire soldier, with the freedom to talk about God and the human soul."

A well-dressed young blond in the back of the room rose to her feet and gestured with her hand.

"Excuse me, Lieutenant, but isn't it true that you used to date Candidate Roberts when you were attending high school?"

The audience burst into laughter, mingled with applause.

Cindy scrunched her brow and laughed. "I beg your pardon?"

"I said, isn't it true you and Candidate Roberts were girlfriend and boyfriend while attending high school?"

"Well, no, we weren't. We may have gone on a few dates, but we were more like friends. Besides, I don't know what that has to do with the center."

A middle-aged woman with dark brown hair rose to her feet.

"Excuse me, but didn't Curtis take you to the senior prom?"

"Yes, we went together. But I still don't see how it relates to this evening. That was ages ago."

A third woman, very young, with dark brown hair with a generous amount of pink tint on one side jumped to her feet.

"Excuse me Candidate Roberts, but were you in love with Lieutenant Quentero when you were younger?"

Curtis leaned close to Cindy as he spoke slowly and clearly. "I believe you fail to consider a lot of things when you are young. As you grow older, hopefully you stop to think things through."

"But did you love her?

Curtis paused and stared toward the back of the room.

"Looking back…yes, I guess I did."

Cindy jerked around in her chair to stare opened-mouth at him, while the audience burst into a mixture of comments, cheers, whistles and applause. Cameras were flashing everywhere. Cindy caught a glimpse of Elizabeth Sparks standing in the back of the room smiling and applauding.

Chapter 12

Edith came from the kitchen with two plates of hot apple pie topped with vanilla ice cream. She handed one to Steven and another to Peter, then returned to the kitchen to bring get two more. She gave one to Cindy and sat on the sofa next to Steven.

"This is good, Mom. Thanks," Peter said over a mouthful.

"You're welcome. Better tell Cindy, though. She hasn't touched hers yet."

Cindy looked up from the pie she had poked with a spoon several times, looking perplexed.

"Don't let it get to you, Cindy," Steven said. "I just meant I didn't know you and Curt had a crush on each other back in high school."

"We didn't," Cindy growled. "I *liked* him, but that was mostly because *all* the girls liked him. He was cute and had a lot of money. I think I only went out with him two, maybe three times, counting the prom. And I only went to the prom with him because neither of us had a date."

"Huh; I didn't think Curt was ever without a girlfriend."

"He had one," she said, finally taking a bite of pie and melting ice cream. "But she got sick and couldn't go. I was the only one available who didn't have a date." She paused to point her spoon and glare at Peter. "And that was because knucklehead asked Jamie Walker to go, and not me."

Peter laughed and dabbed at his mouth with a napkin. "I didn't know you wanted to go with me. Besides, I was elected Prom King and Jamie was the Prom Queen, so naturally I asked her."

"I always wanted to go with you, Pete, even when you were being a pain in the backside."

"Well," Steven paused to take a bite of pie. "It doesn't matter much what the truth is. Everyone is going to believe you and Curt had this great romance going. It's been on every news program all evening, and it'll be on the front page of tomorrow's paper."

"I think it was a set up, but I can't for the life of me figure out why," Edith said.

"That's an easy one." Steven took another spoonful and grinned. "Elizabeth Sparks."

"Liz? Why would Liz do something like that?" Peter said.

"Good press. I hear she's running his campaign now, and Curt's ratings jump every time he's seen with Cindy."

Cynthia set her half-eaten plate on the coffee table and stared at Steven.

"Do you want me to quit talking to him?"

"No...," Steven drug the word out, "just be careful. Politics can get vicious. I just don't want to see you get hurt."

Peter set his plate on the coffee table and helped Cindy as she struggled to climb back into the wheelchair. "Thanks," she said, giving him a weak smile. She turned her chair toward the hallway. "I think I'm gonna be sick." Her voice floated back as she disappeared from sight.

Chapter 13

Cindy stared at the front page of the Modesto Bee over the rim of her coffee mug. Steven was right, as usual. The photographer had captured her expression perfectly right after Curt has said he was in love with her, wide-eyed and open-mouthed.

"Here," Edith said, handing her a page from a tablet.

She glanced at the list of telephone numbers. "What's this?"

"That's the phone numbers of the people who called this morning, hoping to talk to you."

Cindy studied the numbers more closely. There were several from old friends, and one from Doctor Hastings, but she didn't recognize the rest.

"Did they say what they want?"

"Really? Do you need to ask that?"

"No, I don't guess I do, do I?"

After a small breakfast, she returned the call from Doctor Hastings and two more from old friends, and then tossed the list in the trash. She attached a large note to every phone in the house saying, *We're sorry, but Cynthia Quentero is not taking calls today.*

Becky Fowler came by around 1:00 p.m. with a Scrabble board and set it up in the living room.

"Hi there, cowgirl," Steven said as he came through the door and hung his hat on the hat rack.

"I'm a nurse Pop, or haven't you noticed lately?"

"Yeah, I notice more than you think. But I'll bet there's

some nurses who like to ride horses. Besides, I could have been talking to Cindy instead of you." He leaned to kiss her.

"Oh, you're the best dad ever," Becky said, hugging and kissing him back.

"Where are the boys?" Edith asked as she tossed a tray of homemade oatmeal/chocolate chip cookies in the oven.

"Rebuilding the fence next to the highway. Someone didn't apply their brakes until they were about fifty feet into our pasture. It's a good thing the herd was in the next paddock, or we might've had a few head wander onto the highway."

"Do we know who it was?" Edith filled the coffeepot with fresh water and plugged it in.

"Not hardly. I reported it to the Sheriff's Department and our insurance, but we can fix it ourselves cheaper than the deductible." Steven sat in his chair and opened the book he had been reading.

Edith sat down and studied her tiles closely as Cindy positioned her chair at the table.

"So, when do you expect to get the test results?" Edith asked Becky before playing four letters.

"We should have the results sometime tomorrow. Pete and Doctor Hastings will have a look at them and I'll call you with an appointment."

"Well, I hope they tell me I'm going to get out of this stupid chair someday," Cindy said

"Could be," Becky said as she started laying down letters.

Cindy stared at the board open-mouthed as Becky finished her turn.

"You've got some feeling in both legs. I'm not the doctor, but I think that's a good sign. There," she said as she played the last tile, then started counting. "Seventy points."

"You rat! How'd you do that?" Cindy said.

The telephone rang and Edith answered it while Becky drew seven more letters.

Cindy stared at Edith, shaking her head.

No, I don't want to talk to anyone. You're not supposed

to answer.

"Hello?...Yes...and the same to you, Curtis."

Steven closed his book and took a sip of lukewarm coffee, staring at Edith. Becky paused in the middle of placing her new tiles in the holder as Cindy tried in vain to get Edith's attention.

"No, she's not busy. She's right here, playing scrabble with Becky and me. I'll ask."

Edith covered the receiver with her hand.

"Curtis wants to talk to you dear."

Cindy scowled at her." I don't want to talk to anyone Mom."

"It's a perfect time to iron out whatever happened night before last. Here," she held the phone under Cindy's nose.

"Oh, alright!" she hissed as she took the phone.

"Hello, Curt. I hope you're not asking me to attend another one of your fundraisers."

******

Curtis cringed a little at the anger in Cindy's voice. He had discovered her quick temper their senior year at Modesto High, when he tried putting his hands where they shouldn't be in the front seat of his custom Chevy. She slapped him hard enough to leave a perfect bruised imprint of her right hand on his cheek.

"No, and I've already apologized for what happened. I had no idea they would ask questions like that. I hope you will forgive me."

"Yes, Curt, I've forgiven you, but I don't want to attend another event with you."

Curtis chuckled and shook his head. "That's alright. I'm not asking you to. What I would like, if you're willing, is to take you to a nice restaurant and buy you dinner."

"Really?" It was said as more of a statement than a question.

"Yes, really. How about it?

"I don't mean to sound difficult, but why?"

Curtis laughed loudly. "You've always been difficult, Cindy. But I'd like to take you to a nice place where we can get better acquainted. We've got a lot of catching up to do."

Cindy laughed this time. "Really?"

"You've already said that, and yes, really."

Curtis took a deep breath as the line seemed to go dead. He almost hit redial but he could hear Edith Fowler laugh in the background.

"Pleaseeeeeeeeese, Cindy," he pleaded.

"Oh, alright," she said with a laugh. "If you're going to buy me a good steak dinner, I'll go. When?"

"How about this Friday at six? Does that sound alright?"

"Yes, Friday at six will be fine. I'll see you then. Bye."

Curtis placed the telephone in the cradle and smiled at Elizabeth Sparks.

"We're on. I pick her up at 6:00 on Friday."

"I told you she would go," Elizabeth said with a grin. "Now, here's what we're going to do…"

Chapter 14

Curtis was true to his word. His dark blue Cadillac pulled through the gate at exactly five minutes to six and rolled to a stop in front of the house. Curtis got out of the car amid a plethora of barking as Jasper and his friend Sally met him with a friendly greeting. He was dressed in a dark pinstriped suit with a red tie and fought a losing battle keeping the dogs away from the clothes.

"Hey, Jasper, Sally! knock it off!" Steven yelled from the front porch. "Y'all go on now. Go find someone else to pester."

The dogs gave one last bark before dashing toward the barn. Curtis bent over and attempted to brush the dog hair from his pant legs. Steven allowed the screen door to slam shut as he passed Cindy on his way toward the kitchen, mumbling. "What kind of an idiot would wear a wool suit when it's eighty-five degrees outside?"

Curtis rang the doorbell and Cindy yelled as she rolled her chair toward the door. "Bye Mom, Dad. Don't wait up."

Edith cringed as the screen door banged shut a second time. "Bye, honey. Have fun."

******

The parking lot for The Outback Restaurant was packed and Curtis had to make a second pass before pulling into a handicap space near the front door.

"Uh, you're probably going to get a ticket for parking

here," Cindy said, pointing at the sign.

"Not with one of these." He opened the glove box and extracted a handicap sign and hung it on the rearview mirror.

"Really? Where'd you swipe that from?"

"Swipe it? Not me, ma'am." Curtis covered his heart and shook his head. "I'm running for Assembly. I can't afford to swipe anything. People are watching."

Curtis grinned as he opened the door. He used the remote to open the trunk and retrieved her wheelchair. He opened her door and squatted. "May I," he said slipping his arms around her.

"Yes, you may." Cindy slipped her arms around his neck and Curtis lifted her to her chair. "No kidding. Where'd you get the parking permit? She said as he pushed her toward the door.

"I borrowed it from a good friend who has an invalid daughter. I told him we were going out tonight, and he loaned it, as they wouldn't need it this evening."

Curtis wheeled her past the line waiting to get inside. Stopping at the reception counter, he gave the girl his best smile.

"We have a reservation. Curtis Roberts."

"Yes sir, Mr. Roberts. Right this way."

The young girl in uniform gave Cindy the impression she wasn't much over seventeen as she led them to a booth against the back wall in a fairly secluded area from the rest of the restaurant, lighted by candlelight. The only diners she could see from their table were two men seated at a table directly across from them.

"Is this table okay, sir?"

Curtis leaned forward to read the girl's name tag. "The table is perfect, Brittany. Thank you."

Curtis took his time positioning Cindy's wheel chair at the end of the table, then slid into the booth next to her.

Cindy stared at Curtis a long minute before speaking. "Thank you for doing this, Curt. It's actually been a while since I've been inside a nice restaurant."

"Doesn't Bobby ever take you to dinner?"

"Oh, sure. So do Pete and his parents. But if it isn't Mexican, Bobby doesn't consider it food. Pete feels the same. I may *be* Mexican, but I do like a change once in a while."

"I thought so." Curtis smiled sweetly at her. "I remember how you liked good California beef when we were in school. I hear they serve a perfect steak here. You do like steak, don't you?"

"You're kidding, right? That's one of the reasons I like being at the ranch. I get to watch my dinner before it becomes my dinner."

"I thought so." Curtis rested his chin in his palm, elbow against the table, and grinned.

"What's the grin for? You look like the cat that swallowed the canary. What are you thinking?"

Curtis sat up straight and cocked his head to one side.

"Oh, just wondering what would happen if I did something I've been dying to do these past two weeks?"

"And what's that?"

"This." Curtis leaned quickly forward, slipping one arm around her neck and kissed her mouth. At that same instant, the two men seated at the neighboring table swung around holding rapid-speed cameras. Cynthia pulled away with a gasp at the flashes and clicking of the cameras. Curtis pulled back, and growled at them.

"Hey! What are you guys doing? Can't a man and woman have a little privacy?"

One of the men held out one palm in surrender.

"Sorry, sir. We're leaving. It won't happen again."

The men tossed money on the table and vacated in a hurry, leaving their half-eaten meals.

"What in the world do you think you're doing?" Cindy said. "Why did you do that?"

"Do what?" Curtis said.

"Kiss me."

"To be honest, I did it because I wanted to. I've never forgotten the few times I kissed you back in high school."

Cynthia leaned back with a crooked grin and her arms folded across her chest.

"Kissing me wasn't all you tried, if you remember."

Curtis glanced up as Brittany placed two glasses of water on the table.

"Your waitress will be with you shortly."

"Thank you, Brittany."

He waited until the hostess was well out of sight before leaning close to gaze at Cynthia with a solemn expression.

"I know. I was a stupid teenager, and that's what teenagers do. You know? Act stupid." He leaned back and chuckled. "But it isn't like that now, Cindy. Believe me."

"Really?" Cindy giggled. "What is it then? Why the sudden interest, Curt?"

Curtis took a sip of water and cocked his head with a casual grin.

"I honestly don't know. I've always liked you, and then when I saw you in front of the hospital, I felt something I haven't felt in a while. I'd like to see where this leads. What do you think?"

Cindy unfolded her arms and casually spun her glass on the table.

"I never made it any secret that I liked you in high school. I stayed at arm's length, because I knew you weren't kind to some of the girls you dated. You broke a lot of hearts, Curt."

"Yeah, I probably did. Like I said, I was pretty stupid."

They spent a few seconds of silence, gazing at each other. She had to admit Curtis Roberts was one of the best-looking men she had ever seen. He had the real California look. Wavy blond hair and ice-blue eyes with perfect teeth and smile. *Yeah, it wouldn't take much to fall in love with someone like that.*

Curtis took her hand and gently caressed her fingers.

"Look, I'm not going to defend what I did in high school. That was a million years ago and we're adults now. Hopefully, we've grown a little. I know I've changed. I started going to church, and I've turned over a new leaf. I was hoping we might start over by becoming friends. If you don't want this, I'll go away."

Cynthia smiled and squeezed his forearm.

"I appreciate that Curtis. I really do like you, but I want to take it slow. Right now, let's relax and enjoy our dinner. Who knows? We just might become good friends."

She smiled as she tugged on his shirt collar, pulling him closer and planted a small kiss on his lips. It had been awhile since she had kissed a man. Romance between the troops was frowned upon. Besides, it was hard to feel romantic about a battle-buddy who was carrying a M4 and smelled of stale sweat. Curtis, on the other hand, smelled like fresh soap and cologne. His lips were soft and warm.

Curtis smiled and gave her a slightly longer kiss. She slipped her arm around his neck and kissed him again. She never bothered to look toward the cocktail lounge where the two men with the cameras were standing. Fred Nunez lowered his camera and smiled.

"These shots are great! Couldn't have done better if we'd staged them."

Chapter 15

"Ha! Now you've got to king me. Or, should you *queen* me?" Cindy grinned at Peter from the opposite side of the checker board.

"Anybody want a cup of coffee?" Edith said from the kitchen.

"Yeah, I'll take a cup, if you're going to make some," Steven said from the sofa. The 6 o'clock evening news was on the TV.

"No, I don't want any, Mom," Peter studied the board.

"Me neither," Cindy said.

"Hmm, to *king* you, or to *queen* you. That's a good question. Maybe we should call a halt to the game until we can find an answer." Peter reached for a small booklet of game rules.

"Oh no, don't you dare. I'm winning, and we're finishing the game."

Steven Fowler turned up the volume on the television as Elizabeth Sparks appeared on air.

"It seems the denial of a romance between candidate Curtis Roberts and war hero Cynthia Quentero at last week's political fundraiser was not exactly true, as these photographs will show."

Peter froze with a checker in his hand as a photo of Curtis kissing Cynthia appeared on the screen behind Cindy. A second photo appeared, showing Curtis' arm around Cindy's neck and their lips locked.

"These photographs were taken inside the Outback Restaurant in Modesto by fellow diners."

Peter dropped the checker as he stared at the television. Cindy turned her chair to see the screen as the blood drained from her cheeks.

"Well, well. When did this change of heart take place?" Steven said.

"It...it's not what it looks like," Cindy stammered.

"It certainly looks friendly to me, "Edith said with a crooked grin. "Care to tell me about it?"

Peter got up from the table and reached for his jacket.

"Pete?" Cindy said.

"I should be going. I've got a 7:30 appointment with a patient tomorrow morning."

"It's not what it looks like," Cindy repeated as Peter opened the front door.

"See you in a couple of days, Mom."

"Pete? Peter!" Cindy yelled as he closed the door. "Peter! It's not what it looks like!"

"What's it supposed to look like, Cindy?" Steven asked over his cup. "Maybe you can tell us."

She stared at the television screen through misty eyes as the screen switched to a traffic accident.

Chapter 16

Peter sat on the edge of his bed with an open Bible on his lap. He exhaled loudly as he covered his face with both hands.

"Okay God, please help me to be happy for her, if this is what she wants. And you'll need to help me not to hate Curt. God, you know how I feel about her—how much I love her. I always have loved her. But, if you mean for them to be together, then give me the grace to accept it, and to be happy for them."

******

"I can maneuver my own chair, Curt." Cindy said as Curtis started pushing her wheelchair. "I'm not helpless."

"Yes, but I like pushing my girlfriend's chair. I want everyone to know that I really do love you. You don't mind, do you?"

"No...I guess not. Just don't run over anyone."

She sat back in the chair, trying to relax as Curtis wove through the pedestrians at the Vintage Faire Mall. They hadn't gone very far before someone recognized who they were, and wanted to shake hands and talk politics with Curt. It didn't take long before a different group of people were asking her questions and giving her hugs. The day had quickly turned into a campaign rally.

"Well, I thought we might do some window shopping," Curt said when there was a small break in the crowd.

"Window shopping? Since when do men like to

window shop?"

"They normally don't. But that's what women like to do, isn't it?"

"Yes, normally. But we've been here over an hour and we've only been to three stores," Cindy said with a laugh.

"Yeah, but I see a store we can't refuse."

Curtis swung her chair around and headed toward the Dairy Queen. He parked her chair at a small table and grinned.

"Let's see if I remember correctly—it's a chocolate-dipped in a sugar cone."

"Yep, you remember correctly," she said with a grin.

She had a warm feeling inside as she watched Curtis standing in line. *He remembered I like chocolate-dipped cones? What kind of man remembers something like that, unless they really do like you?*

"Excuse me, but you're Cynthia Quentero, aren't you?"

Cindy stared up at the attractive blond holding an infant in one arm, and holding the hand of a small boy with the other.

"Yes, I'm Cindy. What can I do for you? She felt like shouting *go away and leave me alone with my boyfriend*, but instead smiled sweetly.

"My husband lost a leg in Afghanistan and he'll be returning home shortly. I need to know some of the things I can expect. Do you mind?" She motioned toward one of the empty chairs.

Cindy suddenly felt small as the struggling mother took her time seating herself.

"Here," Cindy said, holding both arms toward the boy. "Would you like to sit in my chair with wheels? It can go real fast."

"Yeah!" he said and darted toward her.

Cindy lifted him to her lap. "I'm Cindy. What's your name?"

"Bobby."

"Bobby's a nice name. My brother's name is Bobby." Cindy looked up as Curtis handed her the ice cream cone and added, "Thanks."

"Uh, do I need to buy more?" Curtis' eyes bounced between both women.

"No, thank you," the young mother said. "I just wanted to talk to Miss Quentero."

"Yes, you do," Cindy cut her off. "I'm not going to eat my ice cream in front of a handsome man like Bobby, unless he has one too." She looked at the boy on her lap. "And get one for…I'm sorry; I don't know your name."

"Beth Singleton, but you don't need to buy me ice cream."

"Sure he does. Who doesn't like chocolate dipped cones? And get plenty of napkins." Cindy grinned at Bobby as he bit into her chocolate-dipped cone.

She waited until Curtis got back into the line before turning to Beth.

"I don't know how much help I can give you. I may be crippled, but I still have both legs. There is a difference. He's married and has you and the kids, while I'm still single."

"Yes, but can you at least try? I need to know."

"Sure. It probably won't take long to tell you what I know, but I'll tell you what I've been going through. Will that help?"

Beth nodded, "Thank you."

Cindy began to slowly open her mind and was shocked to see the clock behind the counter had moved forty-five minutes by the time she finished.

"Thank you so much." Beth wiped her eyes. "May I hug you?"

"Sure, hug a way."

"I've got to get these kids home and clean them up." Beth wiped at Bobby's face with a dirty napkin.

"I'll get a wet paper towel," Curtis said and walked briskly toward the men's room.

"In the meantime, I promised Bobby a ride." Cindy backed her chair away from the table and into the middle of the wide walkway.

"Hang on." She slowly began spinning the chair, first to the right, then back to the left. The crowd saw what was happening as Bobby shrieked with giggles. Cindy stopped the spinning and raced in small circles before Beth stopped the fun.

"I'm sorry, but I really have to get home. My parents are coming tonight. Besides, I think you're going to be busy." She pointed toward several small kids staring hopefully.

She started to leave, and then turned back to Cindy.

"May I ask one more thing?"

"Sure, what is it?"

"Could you please pray for us?"

"Okay. I'll put you on my list."

"No, I mean now. Please?"

Cindy paused then took the woman's hand. She prayed softly for God to give her wisdom and patience, and to increase the love and respect they have for each other as husband and wife. When she finished, she gave Beth a hug and kissed her cheek.

"Tell Cindy goodbye," she said to her son.

"Bye." Bobby waved.

"Bye? You can do better than that. Cindy leaned forward and received a sticky kiss.

She waited until Beth had Bobby under control and heading toward the door before turning toward the smiling children.

"Okay, who's next?"

"Me! Me! Me!" Hands went up as they bounced up and down.

"How about you?" Cindy pointed toward a girl with braids.

Curtis pulled his smart phone from his pocket and hit the video command. He had already taken several photographs of Cindy talking to Beth Singleton as well as several minutes of video of her feeding Bobby ice cream and giving him a wheelchair ride. But this was special. He grinned thoughtfully. Liz was right. Cynthia Quentero was special.

Chapter 17

"Yeah, I know how they got there." Curtis raised his eyebrows as he stuffed a French fry into his mouth. Cindy had just asked how the video and pictures of their date at the mall made it to the 6:00 evening news with Elizabeth Sparks.

"Well, I'm waiting."

"She asked if I had taken any pictures of our date, and I handed her my phone." He shrugged. "I thought she was going to download a couple of the photographs. I didn't think she was going to show the video of you giving wheelchair rides. Do you really care?"

They were seated in a booth inside the Farmer Boys restaurant in Riverbank. Besides the fact that they were hoping for a little privacy, she believed they served the best hamburgers ever. Cindy chewed her mouthful of tasty beef and swallowed.

"Well, yeah. I don't know how Beth Singleton feels about having her face and private life plastered all over television. And, her husband might have a problem with it also. Wounded vets, for the most part, are kind of private about certain things." She glared across the table. "Bottom line is…someone should have asked her before using the pictures and video."

"You are absolutely right." Curt dropped his half-eaten burger on the plate and wiped his hands. "She shouldn't have used them, and I'll tell her about it." He cocked his head to one side and shrugged.

"She's new at this. I'm her first candidate."

"Well, I hope she doesn't get you in trouble doing

something like that. Whatever happened to Raymond Chandler anyway?"

"We had a difference of opinion on how to run a campaign and parted ways."

"So, you decided to let Elizabeth Sparks run your campaign?"

"Yeah, that's pretty much it." Cutis nodded. "I got tired of being behind in the polls. Take a look at the numbers." He grabbed his phone and started punching keys. "I've been climbing the ladder steadily. I'm getting real close, and all that's been in the four weeks since she's been running the campaign."

"I don't care about the numbers, Curt. What I care about is you. I don't want to see you get hurt. Someone might get ticked off about her using information and photographs without permission. Do you understand?"

"Sure, sure," he nodded again. "I'll talk to her. What about us? Would you get mad if she posted some pictures of us together?"

"Mmmm, no," Cindy said slowly shaking her head.

"That's good, because I've got a feeling Liz plans on doing just that."

"Really? Why?"

"Because you're a part of me now. People will want to know all about you, same as me."

"Huh, I never thought of it like that." She stuffed another fry into her mouth and looked up as a teenage girl approached their table.

"Excuse me. I saw you on TV last night, giving those children rides in your wheelchair. That was really cute."

"Thank you. I had fun."

"Would you please sign my napkin?" She handed Cindy an unused napkin and a ballpoint pen.

"Sure, I can do that."

"Hey, everyone, this is Cynthia Quentero. She's the one who was on the news last night," the girl yelled as Cindy signed the napkin. In a matter of minutes people were lining up to get autographs and ask questions. Curtis sat back smiling as cameraman Fred Nunez rose from a chair on the opposite side of the restaurant and began taking pictures.

Sweet, Elizabeth. Real sweet, Fred whispered to himself. He never really liked Elizabeth Sparks from the first time he met her. He found her to be arrogant and demanding. She had the looks of a model, and wasn't above using those looks to get what she wanted. But working beside her on Curtis Roberts' campaign was like watching an artist paint a masterpiece. She knew what voters wanted and was giving them exactly what they asked for.

Chapter 18

Fred stormed out of Stanley's office, slamming the door with a bang. Several heads turned to stare silently as he marched to his desk and tossed the day's agenda into the trash. Next, he began clearing the desk and tossing more things into the trash. One of the girls rose from her desk quietly and entered Stanley's office. A few minutes later, producer Stanley Morgan came from his office and sheepishly walked toward Fred, who was still trashing things.

"Fred? Please come back into the office and let's discuss things."

"There isn't anything to discuss, Stan. You pulled the President's speech from me and gave it to Gordon. You promised me that gig three months ago. You even got me security clearance and a press pass. See?" He held the security badge high before tossing it into the trash.

"I know, and I told you why I was making the change. Look," Stanley added after watching Fred toss the contents from the bottom drawer into the overflowing wastebasket. "What's it going to take to make up for the change?"

"You can't," Fred said quietly. "President Trump is only going to give one speech in San Francisco this year. He doesn't get a third term, Stanley. That gig was supposed to be mine. I'm twice the photographer Gordon is, and you know it."

He plopped into the swivel chair and glanced around to make sure he wasn't forgetting anything.

"Well, this isn't the best place to have this discussion. Stop by my office before leaving." Stanley turned and ambled back to his office. A few snickers and snorts erupted as he closed the door. Adam Wright and Harold Martin, two of Fred's colleagues, patted him on the back with words of admiration for his gutsy move.

"Yeah, thanks guys.

******

Fred rapped twice on Stanley's office door before entering. Stanley had cradled the telephone against his shoulder and ear as he looked up from the stack of papers on his desk. Fred placed a company video recorder and a standard Kodak zoom camera on the floor in the corner.

"I'll call you back," Stanley said as Fred turned to leave. He dropped the telephone into the cradle as he motioned toward Fred.

"Please, close the door and sit down. Please," he repeated as Fred glared at him. "Give me five minutes and you can still leave, if that's what you want."

Fred closed the door and sat in the vacant chair without saying a word.

"I know you feel like you've been cheated, but…"

"I don't *feel* I've been cheated, Stan. I *have* been cheated."

"Okay, I agree. The real truth is, we've all been cheated."

"And how's that? I'm the one who had their assignment pulled. What I want is to know why? And I want to hear the truth."

"Okay." The crease between Stanley's eyes deepened. "The truth is I had my orders to pull you and assign you to work beside Elizabeth Sparks on Curtis Roberts' campaign."

"What? Come on, Stanley. We've know each other too long to lie like that. Besides, I've already been photographing his stupid campaign."

"I'm not lying. The owners are in the process of selling the studio, and the ratings have gone up since Liz has been running Curtis' campaign. And a good portion of that jump is due to you and the pictures you've been taking. They feel the president's speech would be a one-time event, but they want to milk Curt's campaign and romance with Cynthia Quentero for all that it's worth. Because," Stanley snickered and shook his head as he poured two cups of coffee, "the more people watching them on the news, means more money in their pockets when the sale finally goes through."

"Really? How does she feel about all this, or does she know?"

"Elizabeth Sparks only knows part of this. All she knows is her campaign seems to be working for Curt Roberts, and her personal popularity is high. And, by the way, it was at her request that you got assigned to her campaign. Don't look so shocked," Stanley added with a chuckle. "She knows you're the best we've got, and she wouldn't be where she is without you."

"Okay, what's in it for me?" Fred said sullenly.

"You get your name plastered on every newscast as the photographer. Equal billing with Liz, so to speak. Plus a 10% raise. That was what I was working on when you came in." He motioned toward the telephone.

Fred sat quietly before giving a firm nod. "Fifteen percent and you've got a deal."

"That might be pushing it a little."

"I've already been working nights and filming his speeches without getting paid extra. They can always try working with Gordon," he added when Stanley glared at him.

"Okay, I'll tell them fifteen percent is your bottom line. Is it a deal?"

"As long as I get my fifteen percent, I'll give them my best."

Fred gave Stanley a half-smile as they shook hands.

Chapter 19

Fred Nunez passed a company credit card to the young girl behind the counter. She had more tattoos than a longshoreman, along with three nose rings. Her orange hair was spiked on one half of her head, and the other half was almost shaved bald.

He had complained when Elizabeth had begged him to follow Curtis Roberts and Cynthia Quentero for the afternoon and take a few pictures. To tell the truth, he was pretty much worn out with politics, especially Elizabeth's style of politics. It was kind of like eating chocolate to the point of wanting to vomit. But seeing the girl behind the counter made up for some of it, plus Stanley had confirmed his fifteen percent raise that morning. Now, the fact he had just ordered a large buttered popcorn, a slice of peperoni pizza and a large Dr. Pepper also helped make up some, especially knowing it was coming out of Elizabeth's budget.

"Thank you," the girl behind the counter said as she returned the card with a receipt.

"You're welcome," Fred said and pulled his camera from his jacket pocket. "Do you mind?" He didn't wait for an answer as the camera clicked twice.

He returned the camera to his pocket and grabbed the cardboard tray holding the pizza and Dr. Pepper.

"I'll make sure you get a copy." He turned away.

"Hey, you some kind of a photographer?" she raised her voice as the next customer took Fred's place.

"Yes, I am, for television news. My name is Fred."

"My name's Zoe."

"I'll bring your picture tomorrow, Zoe."

He hurried toward the theatre as the usher started closing the door. The music had already started.

"Whoa," Fred said rushing forward. "Thanks," he added as the usher let him slip inside. He stood in the back, allowing his eyes to adjust to the dim lighting as he surveyed the sparse audience. He had no idea what movie was playing, and didn't really care. He'd be leaving early anyway.

Fred grinned as he spotted Cynthia's wheelchair, folded and shoved against the end seat on the fourth aisle from the back. True to her word, Liz knew exactly where they'd be sitting. Fred slipped quietly into a seat two rows back and took a sip Dr. Pepper. Placing the cup into the cup-holder, he retrieved his camera. Some woman on the screen was driving a speeding sports car on a country road in a downpour. By the sound of the music, the stupid broad was going to crash real soon. Meanwhile, Cindy had her head resting on Curtis' shoulder and eating popcorn.

He took a bite of pizza and grinned as the driver on screen hit the break pedal, only to discover she had no brakes. Then came the proverbial scream as the car left the pavement and careened off a tree. He aimed and snapped a few photographs as sound of the crash and background music masked the camera's click.

He sat back and finished the pizza as a blue pickup appeared on screen. The driver stopped at the sight of the wreck and pulled the woman from her demolished car. *Must be the hero.* He snapped a couple more photos as a fire truck and ambulance dashed across the screen. Miraculously, the woman who drove the car was still alive.

He waited a half an hour longer and took several more pictures before slipping back into the lobby. He tossed the half-eaten popcorn and Dr. Pepper into the trash. Zoe reached the exit at the same time, causing Fred to grin.

"You didn't like the movie?" she asked. Her smile revealed a tongue stud he hadn't noticed earlier.

"No, I didn't find it that interesting. You getting off

work?"

"Yep. I'm free for the evening."

Up close, and in better lighting, Fred figured he might be twice her age. He normally wouldn't have spoken to her, let alone taken her picture. But, for some reason, he found her extremely interesting, in a crazy sort of way.

"Want to get something decent to eat?" he asked.

"Sure, if you're buying."

"You're on. What do you feel like eating?"

She slipped her arm inside his. "A salad. I'm vegan."

I figured as much. "Okay. Mind if I eat a hamburger?"

"No, just rinse your mouth before you kiss me."

Fred laughed and slipped his arm around her shoulder. "I promise to do that."

Chapter 20

Cindy lay on her back on the living room carpet as Peter took her through her exercises. She could see a sparrow flutter on a low-hanging tree limb outside the window, making her wish she was out there with him. She rolled her head back to stare at Peter. He had just warned her for what seemed the millionth time since she had started seeing Curtis to be careful.

"What makes you think so?" she asked.

"Well" Peter said as he laid her left leg back on the carpet and began stretching her right leg, "Dad's afraid that Curt's not as sincere about your relationship as you are. He wants you to be careful."

"Oh, I didn't know your father was prophet."

"He's not, but he's known the Roberts family for a long time."

"I think Curtis might surprise you both," Cindy said. "He called today just to see how I'm doing. He's sorry about all the media attention we've been getting."

"Really? I thought that was the nature of the political game. Grab all the attention you can."

"Yes, I know what you're thinking," Cindy snapped. "But Curt acts like he really does care about me."

"Maybe. But we know his track record. It isn't exactly clean when it comes to women. He's hurt a lot of girls."

Cynthia propped herself on her elbows and raised her voice.

"Yes, Pete, I know that. And, I've said the same thing to him when all this started. I'm not stupid."

"I never said you were." He held up his hands in

surrender. "Just be careful. That's all I ask."

"I will. He says he's changed, Pete. People do change, once in a while."

Peter laid her leg on the carpet and studied her.

"I didn't come here to argue with you, Cindy. You asked, and I'm just saying Mom and Dad aren't that convinced he's changed much. Frankly, neither am I."

Cynthia glared at him.

"It's only because we love you and care what happens to you".

Cynthia grabbed a cushion from the sofa and gave Peter a whack.

"Hey!" Peter laughed as he tried to shield himself as more blows came.

Cindy spoke through clenched teeth as she kept her assault going.

"Quit – treating – me – like a child. Be happy for me."

"Okay," Peter said, laughing. "I'm happy. I hope you're right. I just think you could find someone better – someone like me."

He laughed as she hit him once more. He slowly began lifting one of her feet toward her head, and then lowered it. He repeated the exercise with the other leg. Peter alternated legs, continuing to stretch her muscles. Somehow, her seeing Curtis Roberts became a forbidden subject.

Chapter 21

"Well, here it is. What do you think?" Fred said, looking much like a child sharing his most treasured possession for the first time. The studio consisted of a small one bedroom mother-in-law apartment sitting at the end of a cracked driveway that skirted the west side of a 1930s two bedroom home in what had at one time been an upscale neighborhood in Modesto.

He had taken Zoe copies of the pictures he took of her behind the counter, and when he had caught her just leaving work. Fred sat beside her on a bench outside the theatre while she looked at the pictures. "They're beautiful," she said, leaning to kiss him on the lips. "Thank you."

"You're welcome. Are you free this evening?"

"Yes. I just need to take a shower and change clothes." She plucked at the front of her uniform and sniffed the sleeve. "I smell like buttered popcorn."

"There's worse things to smell like, but I can wait. Where's your car?"

"It's right over there." Zoe pointed toward a fairly new black Camaro parked directly across from where they were seated.

"Nice," Fred said, taking her arm. "I need to ask for another raise, if you can own a Camaro while working behind the counter at the theater."

"Don't I wish," Zoe said with a snort. "You're looking at the wrong car."

She led him past the Camaro to where a beat up white

Chevy with a black front fender and hood sat. Fred gave an involuntary shudder. He'd seen better looking vehicles at crash sites.

"Could you follow me home? My car isn't running too well."

"Sure. I'm parked right over there." He pointed toward the row to their left. He walked briskly toward his car as Zoe cranked the engine. He gave kudos to the battery in her car. She was still cranking the engine when he slid into his car and snapped the seatbelt closed. Her car started with a loud cough and a cloud of blue smoke. Fred had never thought of himself as a mechanic by any stretch of his imagination, but he believed Zoe's old Chevy needed to be put out of its misery.

He waited while she rolled past and turned right out of the parking lot. He held his breath as the cloud of smoke from her car engulfed him as she accelerated. There wasn't any need to ride her bumper since she was leaving a trail of smoke. He fell a half a block back and followed the smoke. He was still a quarter of a block behind her when she parked in front of a shabby house on Paradise Avenue, in one of the worse neighborhoods in Modesto. He had done some filming for the news in the area, and took time locking his car as Zoe bounded inside.

From the sound of things, he doubted he'd see her the rest of the evening. A man and a woman were exchanging heated words, and he believed getting involved might not be the wisest thing he could do. He leaned against the right front fender of his car and studied the house. The front screen door hung catty-wumpus from one hinge. There were several dozen empty cans and bottles scattered about the porch and yard. What little grass there was was dry and yellow. He jerked as a loud crash echoed from inside as someone threw something. He hadn't really kept track, but he believed he had heard more profanity in the short time he'd been there than when he was called to film inside a biker bar after someone had been stabbed.

To his surprise, Zoe came bounding out, still dressed in

her work clothes and carrying a plastic grocery bag stuffed with clothing. Fred unlocked the doors and she slid inside the passenger side as another crash sounded inside the house.

"I'm sorry about that," she said glaring at the windshield. Fred started his car and pulled away from the curb.

"Who was that fighting inside the house?"

"My mom and her boyfriend. They get drunk and do that a lot." She exhaled slowly. "You really don't have to take me anywhere, if you don't want. I understand."

"Understand what?"

"That guys like you don't date girls like me."

"Really? I didn't know that," Fred said with a chuckle.

"Don't make fun of me," she snapped.

"I wasn't…"

"Stop the car and let me out!"

"Zoe…"

"Stop the car!"

Fred pulled to the curb and threw the car into park. Zoe fumbled for the door handle as Fred grabbed her and planted a kiss on her lips. She broke the kiss to stare at him for a few seconds.

"Really?"

"Yes, really."

"Why?"

"I wasn't lying when I said I found you fascinating, Zoe. I like you a lot. I can't explain it, but I do. You can believe me. I promise I won't lie to you."

She giggled as she slipped her arms around his neck. "Now, that would make you different from all the other guys." She pulled him close and kissed him. It was his cell phone that broke the spell with the sound of James Brown screaming, "I Feel Good."

"Well," he said reading the message. "I hope you don't mind a slight change in plans. I've been called in to work."

"Really? I can walk home from here."

"Why? You can go with me. Elizabeth wants me to take a few pictures at Curtis Robert's political thing at the park tonight. It doesn't start for a couple of hours, so I'll show you my studio and you can shower and change there, if you want. Then," he shrugged as he turned onto J Street, "I'll fix you dinner. Sound good?"

"Yes, it does." She slipped her hand into his and squeezed.

******

Zoe came from the bathroom in bare feet drying her hair. They had gone to Curt's event where Fred quickly took a dozen photographs before grabbing Zoe by the hand and rushed toward the car.

"Did you find everything?" he asked.

"Yes, I did." She smiled at him. "I love your bathroom. Your shower actually works, and you have hot water."

"Yes, that's two things I am rather fond of."

"Do you actually own this place?"

Fred laid the photograph he was studying back on the coffee table and grinned at her. "Yes, it belonged to my grandmother. She gave it to me in her will. I'd rather have her than the house, but I'm thankful anyway."

He stared out the kitchen window and heaved a sigh remembering Grandma Beth. He'd never known either of his parents. Grandma Beth was the only parent he had known, and he missed her terribly.

"I want to turn the apartment into a studio and quit my job at the station, but it all takes money."

"It's a real nice place. I love it," Zoe said. "Is that what you do for a living? You know, what you did tonight? Take pictures of speeches and stuff?"

"Yeah, if that's what they want. Sometimes I photograph accidents, fires, robberies. I've filmed a couple of murder scenes."

"Really?

"Yes, and they weren't very pretty."

Zoe leaned over to towel dry the half of her head that

had hair and paused as she looked out the dining room window.

"Quick. Give me your camera."

"Sure. Why?"

Zoe grabbed the small Kodak and quietly stepped onto the porch. She squatted to photograph a bumble bee drinking from a red rose next to the house.

"Sorry," she said handing him the camera. "I just thought that would make a good picture."

"I think you're right." Fred plugged the camera into his laptop and found the picture. "See? You were right."

Zoe draped her arms around Fred's neck from behind and placed her cheek next to his. "It is pretty, isn't it?"

"Yes, but let's see what it looks like like this." Fred clicked the mouse a couple of times and the photograph turned black and white. "What do you think?"

"Oh, wow! How'd you do that?"

"Computer magic, my dear. But the real magic is your eye, Zoe. Most people would never have thought of taking the picture in the first place. You've got natural talent. You'd make a great photographer."

She was still studying the picture on the computer when Fred slid two plates and silverware onto the table. "I hope you're hungry. Because…" He pulled a large bowl of garden salad from the refrigerator. "I don't want to have to eat all this myself."

"Great, I'm starved."

"By the way," Fred said as he set two tumblers of water on the table. "How old are you?"

"Nineteen. Why? Does that make a difference?"

"No, just curious." He grinned as he slid one of the tumblers next to her plate. "I'm twenty-seven. Does that make a difference with you?"

"Only that you act like a man and not a kid. Now, can we eat?"

"Dig in."

It was three hours later when Fred turned the television off with the remote, and gently laid Zoe's head on the sofa. He had never considered letting her spend the night at his house, but taking her back to that house might jeopardize her life. He covered her with a light blanket and paused to study her face. She had not replaced the nose rings or Goth makeup. Zoe Shultz was beautiful. He gently kissed her cheek and dimmed the light before disappearing into the bedroom.

Chapter 22

Peter tossed his half-eaten hot dog in the trash as the band quit playing. It took him a couple of minutes to worm his way under a shade tree where he could see the entire stage. Whatever Elizabeth Sparks had been doing seemed to be working. A fairly large crowd had gathered in front of the flag-draped stage to hear one of Curt's speeches. Attending the event was the last thing Pete planned on doing. He would rather have had a root-canal.

To be honest, he had never liked Curtis Roberts in all the years he'd known him. The *why* was something he'd never allowed himself to dwell on. Maybe it was because Curt was born with every advantage possible, yet chose to take the easy way to get what he wanted. He had never balked at telling half-truths or even a blatant lie, if he thought it was to his advantage.

Pete glared toward the stage. There was Cindy, seated in her wheelchair in full uniform, beside and slightly behind Curt as he tore into his opponent. Cindy applauded something he had said as Pete turned away. He walked quickly toward his truck without looking back. The empty hole in his chest was deeper than ever. It was the exact size of the girl in the wheelchair.

The Valley of Decision

Chapter 23

Cynthia leaned over the collection of papers piled on top of the desk shoved against the living room wall. Her left elbow was propped against the desk as her left hand rubbed her crinkled forehead. Edith Fowler stopped her vacuuming to stare at her a couple of seconds.

"What's the matter, dear? You look perplexed."

"I am." She looked up and shook her head. "I promised Pop I would help him with some of the bookwork, but I can't make heads or tails out of his system."

Edith laughed as she crossed the room to stare at the messy desk.

"Now you understand why I never go near that desk. I tried keeping books when he first took over the ranch from his father. I couldn't understand his father's system and I can't understand Steve's system either. He used to get angry when I offered suggestions."

"How does he ever do the taxes?" Cindy asked with an air of frustration.

"He doesn't. We hire it done, and I'm sure they hate seeing us coming. Steve just dumps several large envelopes stuffed with pieces of paper on their desk and leaves."

"That must get expensive."

"Oh, it does," Edith said with a nod. "I've told him we could save a lot of time and money if everything was in order."

They both turned as the door opened. Peter entered carrying a new cowboy hat. A grin crept across his face as he crossed the room to look over Cynthia's shoulder.

"I could have warned you. Trying to make sense of dad's *system* will cause you to take up drinking."

Cynthia eyed the new hat and shifted to study his face.

"Buy yourself a new hat? What's the occasion?"

"No, I actually bought the hat for you. And the occasion is, we're going riding."

"Riding?" Cindy said with a smirk.

She heaved a heavy sigh as she turned back to the messy desk.

"I don't think I'll be doing any more horseback riding, Pete. Thanks for the offer."

Peter turned to his mother.

"Did I say *horseback riding*, mom?"

"Mmm, no, not that I recall. I really wish you two would vacate the living room, so I can finish vacuuming."

"Okay, fine with me," Peter said. He grabbed Cynthia's chair and pulled it away from the desk. He put the hat on her head and wheeled the chair toward the front door.

"Hey," she yelled, locking the break. "What are you doing? I promised your father I'd do something with his desk."

"That's impossible," Pete said, releasing the break. "You can't do anything with the desk without changing the way dad thinks."

He opened the door and wheeled her onto the front deck. A horse hitched to an antique buggy stood in the driveway.

"Your chariot awaits, my dear," Pete said with a wave of his arm.

"Oh, wow! Where in the world did you find that?"

Peter wheeled her down the ramp toward the buggy.

"I bought it from Manuel Ramos this morning. He's had it sitting inside a barn for years. I guess he must have gotten tired of hearing me beg, so he called and said I could have it as long as I bought Pedro."

Peter locked the chair brake and bent to slip one arm behind Cynthia's back and the other arm under her legs. She slipped an arm around his neck as he carried her from the chair to the buggy.

"Is Pedro the horse?"

"Yeah." He paused to look at her. "He's trained to pull the buggy. I'm sure you've seen them before. I think they've been in every parade in the valley." He stared at her a moment longer before she cleared her throat.

"Do you mind?"

"Ah, no."

He placed her inside the buggy and climbed in the opposite side as Edith joined them.

"That looks like fun. I hope you're planning on taking your mother for a ride when you get back."

"I think Cindy will be able to take you riding when we get back."

"Me?" Cindy said. "I don't know how to drive a buggy."

"It's not that hard. In fact, it's rather easy."

Peter handed her the reins.

"Hold them in your hands like this, with the straps through your fingers. We'll have to dig up your old riding gloves. Now, you're set."

Peter grinned as he adjusted the brim of her hat.

"Okay, give the reins a shake and tell him to go."

Cindy gave the reins a gentle shake and yelled. "Ya! Get up, Pedro."

The horse started forward at a trot.

"Okay," she looked up at Pete, "how do I turn?"

Peter reached over to hold her hands.

"Pull back on the left rein, if you want to turn left, and pull on the right, if you want to go right. Pull back on both when you want to stop."

He let go of her hands and she gave the reins another shake and yelled.

"Ya! Come on Pedro. Move!"

The horse broke into a faster gate and the buggy rolled smoothly on the freshly graded field road.

"Hey, this is fun. Thank you so much for doing this for

me," Cindy said.

"My pleasure, ma'am," Pete said with a John Wayne drawl. "I thought you would enjoy it."

Chapter 24

Steven bumped the volume on the TV up as Elizabeth Sparks' image appeared on screen. Cindy closed the magazine she'd been reading and tossed it on the end table.

"I wonder what she's going to say tonight," Edith said with a chuckle.

"The romance between Curtis Roberts and war hero Cynthia Quentero seems to be heating up, as these photographs will show."

"I wish she would quit calling me that." Cindy scowled. "Everybody that's been sent over there is a hero."

"She won't," Steven said. "It's good press and collects votes."

"Shhhh, you two," Edith said. "I want to hear what she's saying.

A photo of Curtis pushing Cindy's wheelchair through the mall appeared on screen.

"Candidate Roberts left the campaign trail to do a little shopping with what appears to be his new sweetheart."

The photo quickly changed to Cindy and Curt inside the Farmer Boys restaurant eating hamburgers.

"There's nothing like a cheeseburger and fries to prove what Candidate Roberts has been saying all along. He's the representative of the middle-class working man and woman. It appears Miss Quentero is also."

A picture of them inside the theatre appeared.

"Of course, when you're in love, there's always time for a good movie and popcorn."

"My, my, is there something we should know?" Steven

asked.

"No." Cindy shook her head and pointed toward the TV. "I didn't know we were being photographed. I never saw anyone with a camera anywhere."

"Well, don't let it get your goat," Edith said, patting Cindy on the arm. "I have to agree with what Peter said the other day. As long as you're seeing Curt, you'd better get used to having your picture taken or a microphone shoved in your face. Politicians don't really have a private life."

"I'm not a politician."

"No, but you're seeing one."

******

Cindy guided her chair down the ramp and out onto the front lawn. The warm sun felt good on her back. The absence of a ringing telephone felt even better. She had unplugged every phone in the house without telling Edith, and turned her own cell phone off.

Jasper saw her from the barn and trotted over to drop a slobbery tennis ball in her lap.

"Okay," she said, giving the ball a toss. "The things I do for a cute border collie." Jasper returned the ball and she gave it another toss as a fairly new BMW rolled to a stop in the driveway and Dr. Hastings climbed out. Jasper dropped the ball in her lap again as the doctor headed her way.

"Not now, Jasper. Let's see what the doctor wants." She patted the dog on the head as Edith came through the door wiping her hands on a dish towel and smiling.

"Hello, Randy. How did Cindy's tests come out? Is everything okay?"

"Hi, Mrs. Fowler. Yes, everything is fine, and the results didn't show anything to be concerned with. Speaking of which, we haven't done any tests on you in a while. In fact, you haven't been inside my office other than to bring Cindy. You're way overdue for your mammogram. I've scheduled an appointment for you next Thursday at 2:00 p.m. Don't miss it."

"I take it my son sent you out here to scold me."

"Something like that," Randy said with a grin and a nod. "Don't forget. Thursday at 2:00.

"Thursday?" Edith said thoughtfully. "I don't know, Randy. I think I have something scheduled at that time. I'll have to check and get back to you."

"Edith Fowler!" Randy raised his voice and shook a finger in her face. "Drop whatever it is and get your mammogram! I mean it."

"Do you know how much they hurt?" Edith crossed her arms across her breasts.

"They can't hurt half as bad as breast cancer." He turned toward Cynthia.

"Where's that ignorant colleague of mine? I heard he took the afternoon off from the hospital."

"He's out with Pop doing something with the cattle. She threw the tennis ball and Jasper bolted after it.

"What do you want to see him for? I thought you were coming to see me."

Randy took the ball when Jasper returned and gave it a long toss. "I did come to see you. I just wanted to rub his nose in the pictures of you kissing Curt."

Cindy covered her eyes with a hand and shook her head. "Please, not you too. The telephone hasn't stopped ringing all day. That's why I'm out here with the dog. At least he doesn't ask a bunch of stupid questions. Is there anything you'd like to add to the zillions of things I've already heard?"

"No, you're a big girl," Randy said. "You can take care of yourself. At least I think you can. Just be careful and pray about it. It hasn't been that long since Curt's had a small harem at his fingertips."

Cynthia grabbed the ball and gritted her teeth as she gave it a throw. The ball bounced off a small tractor and across the hood of Randy's car.

"Oh, sorry about that. But Curt says he's changed. He said he started going to church."

"Ah-hah," Randy said with a nod. "The famous code

words?"

"What code words?" She turned her chair slightly to glare in his face.

"*Going to church.* That's supposed to mean he's changed. The last time I checked, the devil attends church every Sunday. The real question is, did Curt repent and accept Christ as his savior?"

"Your point is well taken, Doctor. Is there anything else?"

"Yes, keep doing whatever you and Pete are doing with your exercises. The tests didn't show anything new, but if you're getting some feeling back into your feet, something's going on. I'd like to see you again on Thursday. We might see if you can stand for a few seconds."

He reached into his shirt pocket and handed her a card.

"Here's your appointment. Yours and Edith's both. And please don't try standing on your own. I don't want you to fall and get banged up."

He turned toward his car and waved to Edith on the porch.

"Bye, Mrs. Fowler. Don't forget your appointment. I took the liberty of making it the same day as Cindy's, so you only have to make one trip to town."

He opened the car door and paused.

"By the way, your telephones aren't working. You know that, don't you?"

"No, I didn't. Thank you." Edith turned toward Cindy as Dr. Hastings drove away.

"Cindy, do you know anything about our telephones not working?"

Chapter 25

Edith Fowler sat back and kicked her shoes off before resting her feet on her footstool. Steven adjusted the volume on the television as anchor woman Rita Lorenzo was interviewing Elizabeth Sparks on the 6 o'clock news.

"These figures are pretty amazing, Elizabeth. The way the gap between the two candidates has closed is nothing short of a miracle."

"Yes, I agree," Elizabeth said with a nod. "Given the margin of error, it's a dead heat. It wouldn't surprise me if Curtis Roberts jumps ahead in the polls sometime next week."

"Most everyone has known for a while that Curtis and his former campaign manager, Raymond Chandler, did not see eye to eye on a number of issues. And I understand that you are now running his campaign. What have you done that has made this change?"

"Actually, I haven't made any changes, except for encouraging Curtis to be himself," Elizabeth said with a perfect smile toward the camera. "I believe that the voting public will flock to him, once they get to know the real Curtis Roberts."

"Thank you, Elizabeth. Whatever you are doing seems to be the right things as far as Candidate Roberts is concerned."

Elizabeth's image disappeared and Rita began talking about the local housing market.

"Curtis Roberts being himself," Edith said absently.

"Now, that's a scary thought," Steven said.

"Makes me wonder who and what he's been all this time," Edith said.

******

Curtis stood at the back of the sanctuary scanning the congregation, trying desperately to find the Fowlers before the service started. The PA system was playing a medium tempo contemporary hymn that he thought had a catchy beat, even if he didn't recognize the tune. He stepped aside in order to allow several people in front of him to find their seats. He smiled and nodded toward them. He spotted Cindy's chair and headed toward the front of the building.

I should've known. She's probably the only wheelchair-bound person in the world that would sit on the front pew.

Curtis stopped at Cynthia's chair and smiled at Peter, who was seated next to her.

"Would you mind scooting over, so I can sit next to this lovely lady?"

Peter looked at him in surprise, but scooted over, causing his parents and Becky to shift. Curtis squeezed in next to Cynthia and smiled at her.

"I didn't expect to see you here," Cindy said.

"Really? I told you I started going to church."

"Yeah, but I've never seen you in this one. Where do you normally attend?"

"I attend Bethel with my parents. But, I heard you came here, so I thought I'd join you this morning. You don't mind, do you?"

"No, I don't mind if you go to church Curtis," Cindy said with a laugh.

The church got suddenly quieter as a group of people appeared from back stage and took their places behind several instruments and microphones. A young man counted off a beat and the worship team began playing. The entire congregation stood and joined in the song. When the song finished, the young man led in an opening prayer, followed by several more songs.

Curtis stood and joined in the singing. He glanced at Cindy from time to time, wondering how someone who had studied her Bible and prayed daily could still sing and praise the same God who allowed her to be crippled.

******

Curtis hung back following the service and practically begged Cindy to let him push her chair.

"I'll repeat what I told you at the mall, Curt. I *can* wheel my own chair and get around pretty good."

"I know you can, but it just seems a little safer in this crowd. Besides, I feel lucky when I have the chance to do something for you."

"Okay, if you want to push me that bad, go ahead," she said with a shrug, "just don't run over anyone."

Peter shook hands and said hello to several people, but spent most of the time it took to exit the building glaring at the back of Curtis' head, wishing he had Superman's x-ray vision so he could melt Curt's skull. Curtis had pushed Cynthia's chair clear of a group of people, when Elizabeth's photographer, Fred Nunez, appeared from the group to snap several pictures. A young girl with spiked hair slipped up beside him, pointing her smart phone at Cindy.

Steven laughed as he leaned toward Peter.

"I could've guessed that was going to happen. Wanna bet a hamburger and fries those pictures aren't going to appear on tonight's news?"

"No, Pop," Peter said with a laugh. "I wouldn't take that bet."

******

"Get out of jail free," Cynthia said as she turned the card over. "I could've used that a few minutes ago."

"Maybe, but you're still ahead," Peter said, shaking the dice in the cup.

Edith came from the kitchen with several cups of steaming coffee on a tray and set it on the coffee table. Steven reached for the remote to adjust the volume as Elizabeth Sparks' image filled the screen.

"Here you are, folks, if you want to see yourself on television." Steven grabbed one of the cups of coffee and sat back in his recliner.

"Conservative state candidate Curtis Roberts decided to attend First Baptist in Modesto today with his friend Cynthia Quentero."

The television screen switched to a video showing Curtis pushing Cynthia.

"Whoa," Edith said with a chuckle. "I didn't see any video cameras. Did you?"

"Not me," Steven said. "But they use cell phones now. It would be easy to miss someone filming you."

"I think it was that girl with all the tattoos and piercings," Peter said as he turned Cindy's chair so she could see the TV better.

"Think so?" Steven asked. "That girl had more hardware stuck to her than my John Deer tractor."

"Steven," Edith said with a scowl.

"Well, it's true."

"Anyway," Peter said, "she had a cell phone pointed our way the whole time, so I'd say it was her." Peter handed Cindy a cup of coffee.

"I think you'd better be prepared to have your picture taken any time you're with Curt."

"What's that supposed to mean? A small crease appeared between Cindy's eyes.

"Nothing, except they seem to be getting a lot of mileage out of showing you and Curt together. It's still a month to the election, so get used to having your picture taken. That's all."

Chapter 26

"I hate to think of it, but we'd better be heading toward the barn," Peter said, checking his watch. "I need to get a couple of hours sleep before heading to the hospital."

Cindy frowned as she slowed the buggy. "You're on duty tonight?"

"Yeah, they were short a GP, so I got the call."

"They're always short," Cindy grumbled as she turned the buggy around. Peter grinned as she shook the reins. She held the reins and handled the buggy like an old pro.

"Yaa! Get up there, Pedro. Move it!" she yelled and shook the reins harder. Cindy and Peter laughed as the horse began to run. The buggy sped over a small hill and toward the ranch house.

Cynthia pulled back on the reins and applied the brake as she brought the buggy to a halt in front of the house.

"Whoa, Pedro. Whoa."

Peter jumped out to get Cynthia's wheelchair that was parked by the driveway. He paused as Miguel came from the barn to hold Pedro's halter. Peter took one look at Miguel's somber face and stopped.

"Hey, what's wrong?"

"Better ask them." Miguel nodded toward the house. Peter turned toward the house as Cynthia leaned out to see the front porch.

Steven and Edith Fowler were both on the porch, and it was obvious, even at that distance, that Edith had been crying.

Peter helped Cindy into her chair. "Come on, we'd better see what happened." He rolled the chair up the ramp and stopped in front of his parents.

"Mom? Dad? What's wrong?"

"Mrs. Wilson called while you were gone," Edith said as she wiped her eyes. "She said Gary was killed yesterday."

"Oh God! No, no, no, no!" Cindy sobbed.

Edith and Peter knelt beside Cindy's chair and hugged her while she cried. The Wilsons were close friends, and Gary had seemed more like a brother to Peter and Cindy than anything else. Peter pulled back after a minute to stare at his father.

"He only had a few months to go. How did it happen?"

Steven gave a little shrug. "It happened on base. Gary's dad said some Afghan soldier they were training went ballistic and started shooting. He wounded six before killing Gary. One of our Seals killed him before he could hurt any others."

Seth pulled into the driveway in the Fowler company pickup loaded with hay. He got out of the truck slowly and stared at the scene on the front porch. Steven waved at the young men, motioning them onto the porch.

"Seth? You and Miguel both come here. Gary got killed yesterday, and we need to pray for his family, especially his mother."

******

It took a week for Gary Wilson's body to arrive in Modesto, then two more days for the funeral arrangements to be made. The pastor of the Baptist church the Wilson's attended delivered a rousing sermon that stirred the majority of the congregation to tears and instilled pride in their hearts toward their fallen hero.

Most of the worshipers followed the hearse to the cemetery where Gary's flag-draped casket was placed in front of the mourners seated in folding chairs. A military color guard was standing by with several soldiers armed with rifles.

Cynthia was clothed in her full-dress uniform. She spied Curtis standing next to Elizabeth at the edge of the medium-sized crowd. Fred, the cameraman Elizabeth liked to use, was standing beside them and filming the service. Peter parked Cindy's chair up front, one row behind Gary's parents, and sat beside her.

Gary's pastor read a few verses from 2 Corinthians about believers being translated in the "twinkling of an eye" and being caught up into heaven with Jesus. Then, after a short prayer, he stepped back and a uniformed officer stepped forward. Cynthia struggled to stand as they began folding the flag. She turned to Peter after a couple of failed attempts.

"Help me. Hold me up. Please!"

Peter nodded toward Seth and they helped her to her feet, holding her upright as she saluted the coffin. She held her salute as the order for the twenty-one gun salute was given.

Elizabeth grabbed Curtis by the arm and leaned on her tiptoes to whisper in his ear.

"You're wasting a ton of good publicity. Get up there and help hold her up."

"But Pete's already..."

"I don't care what Pete's doing. Get up there...now!"

She turned to Fred as Curtis hurried down the isle.

"Keep the camera on Cindy, and make sure you get some good film of Curt holding her up."

Cynthia stood ramrod straight with tears streaming down her cheeks as the bugler started playing Taps. Curtis slipped up behind to take hold of the back of her jacket and grin toward Fred holding the camera. Peter glanced toward him, and then turned back toward the proceedings. Curt's grip on her uniform wasn't helping hold her upright, but Elizabeth was right. It should look great on camera.

Peter and Seth helped Cindy back into her chair and Curtis disappeared as quickly as he had arrived. Cindy rolled her chair forward to offer her hand to Mrs. Wilson, but instead got embraced by both of Gary's parents. She slowly broke the embrace as the mourners began to file past the casket.

Peter stood to one side, waiting for his chance to offer his condolences to Mr. and Mrs. Wilson. *"Good Lord have mercy,"* he said under his breath. Elizabeth Sparks was positioning Curtis behind Gary's coffin, and they were filming him as he began a speech.

Chapter 27

Edith came from the kitchen holding a tray with cups of coffee. She set the tray on the coffee table and glanced around. Steven and Peter were sitting quietly, staring at the local news on the television.

"Is Cindy still in her bedroom?"

"Yeah," Peter said absently. "I knocked to see if she was alright, and she said she was tired and going to rest."

Edith handed Steven and Peter cups of coffee and took one for herself. She sat in her favorite chair and glared at the television. The sound of a bugle playing Taps floated from the speaker as the camera slowly panned the mourners. Everyone inside the cemetery had somber expressions, except Curtis, who kept smiling at the camera.

"No wonder she's tired," Edith said with a growl. "That was quite a dog 'n pony show Curt put on. I never thought he'd stoop that low. Simply disgraceful!"

She took a sip of coffee and set the mug back on the table with a thud.

"Especially at a service for someone he was supposed to be friends with."

Peter snorted and shook his head.

"I don't know where you got that idea, Mom. He never hung around anyone like Gary. Curt ran with a different crowd."

"Why? What's wrong with Gary?" Steven asked.

"Nothing except he was poor and black." Peter took a sip of coffee.

"What's that got to do with anything?" Steven scowled.

"He ate at our table many a time, and I don't have a clue how many times he slept in the guest bedroom. The color of his skin didn't rub off. Besides, Cindy and Bobby are Mexican, and he's claiming to be in love with her."

"You'd have to ask him that question, Pop. As far as him being in love with Cindy…" He shrugged. "That was news to me also. I knew she had a crush on him, and I know he took her on a couple of dates. But he seemed to be more interested in seeing how far she'd go. I understand he tried getting cute one night and she slapped his face. He never asked her out again."

"How come you've never said any of this before? And how come you and Bobby didn't teach him a lesson?" Steven scowled.

"We were going to, but Cindy stopped us. She said she was big enough to take care of herself."

They turned their attention back to the television as Curtis' face appeared on the screen. He was being interviewed by Elizabeth while the mourners slowly made their way toward their cars. He was saying something about how the war is being mishandled.

"And I suppose he knows how to run a war?" Steven almost yelled. "He's never worn a uniform of any kind. And he's running for a state office. He's making it sound like he's running for president."

"Well, regardless, he certainly lost my vote today," Edith said quietly.

Peter took a sip of coffee and chuckled.

"Don't tell Cindy. She seems to think the sun rises and sets in him."

Chapter 28

Cindy bolted through the opened door and hugged the Humvee with her shoulder as she crept forward. The gunfire coming from the hillside cast a shower of bullets that rattled loudly against the side of the vehicles. The first RPG had disabled the lead Humvee and blocked the roadway. A second RPG had disabled the rear vehicle, stranding the rest in the middle.

"Anyone see where that came from?" Captain Miller yelled.

"From the top of the ridge, sir!" Cindy yelled.

Captain Miller turned to grab the microphone from the cab of the Humvee when a bullet ricocheted off the opened door with a loud crack, knocking him to the ground.

"Captain! Captain," Cindy said as she knelt beside him. "Come on, now, stick with me," she said, slapping his face. "Speak to me. Captain!"

She cradled his head in her hands as she yelled for a medic. She could feel Captain Miller's warm blood cover her hands as it oozed from the hole at the base of his skull. She yelled for a medic twice more. She tried stemming the flow of blood with her fingers as she watched Gary Wilson and another medic she did not know approach. She could tell they were running, but never got any closer. It was like watching a film in slow motion.

"Come on…hurry!"

Then, Captain Miller's head detached itself from his body and she dropped it in the dirt. The head rolled to her knees as she tried scrambling to her feet. Captain Miller's eyes locked on her face as he said, "Help me, Lieutenant."

******

Cindy bolted upright in her bed screaming.

"No! No! God, please help me! Oh, God, no!"

Edith rushed into the bedroom with Steven at her heels. Edith grabbed for Cynthia only to get hit in the face by her fist. Steven pulled Edith away and grabbed Cindy, pinning her arms to her side.

"Shh, shh, it's okay, it's okay! You're safe now. We're here with you. It's okay."

Cindy jerked her head back to see Steven then burst into tears with her head on his shoulder.

"You're safe, honey." Steven said. "You're safe."

******

Peter took a sip of coffee and set the cup on the kitchen table. "You should have called me last night," he said as he studied Edith's swollen and bruised eye.

"Why? There wasn't anything you could've done that I didn't do myself. Besides..." she scrunched her eyes as Peter pressed around the bruised area.

"That hurts, doesn't it?" he said.

"Well, yes, with you poking at it." She swatted his hand away. "As I was saying, before you decided to torture your mother, it was the middle of the night. Do you like getting awakened in the middle of the night?"

"No, but you're special. You're my mother, and I *want* you to call whenever there's a problem."

"You both are forgetting something," Cindy said.

"And, what's that, dear," Edith asked.

"I was the one who belted you, and that really looks nasty. I'm really, really sorry."

"That's quite alright. I should have known better than to disturb you in the middle of a nightmare."

"And how were you supposed to know that?" Peter applied a dab of salve over the small cut. "Besides, waking her might be a good thing. She could hurt herself acting out another dream."

He studied Cindy for a moment. "How many dreams like this have you had?"

"Only a few," but none where Captain Miller's head came off in my hands and spoke to me."

"And how bad were the others?"

"Gee, I don't know. We were shooting at each other, and people were getting blown up. How bad do you want it to be?

"What I'm trying to determine is if last night's dream was worse than the others, or were they about the same?"

Cynthia sat quietly for a few minutes before answering.

"Last night's dream was worse. The helicopter didn't show. I could hear him, but he was lost somewhere, trying to find us. I could see Gary and the other medic running toward us, but they never got any closer." Her voice broke and she covered her mouth with her hand.

"That's what I thought," Peter said and pulled a card from his shirt pocket. "I want you to call this number and make an appointment to talk to her."

"I can get counseling through the V.A., Pete," Cindy said with a snort.

"I know you can, but that might take months. I really want you to talk to her."

"That costs money. How am I supposed to pay," she glanced at the card, "Deborah Mills for her time?"

"The first visit is free. Talk to her and we'll discuss any future visits after that."

Peter stared at her quietly as a grin crept across his face.

"I know it's a pain, Cindy, but do this for me. Please?"

"Okay, but it might be better to warn everyone on the ranch to stay out of my room if they hear me yelling or raising a fuss in the middle of the night."

Chapter 29

Cindy adjusted a set of ear protectors then moved her wheelchair next to a stand in an outdoor shooting range. Deborah Mills had proven herself to be the expert counselor Pete promised her to be.

"She believes the dream was brought on by Gary's death and funeral. The fact that Gary died and I wasn't there to help when he needed me caused me to feel helpless. It all sounds reasonable enough. I don't know, maybe she's right," she said with a shrug.

"So, when do you see her again?" Peter asked.

"I didn't make another appointment."

"Why not?"

"There's a little thing called money. I warned you," she added as Peter shook his head.

"Well, neither of you said anything at all to *me* about this," Steven said.

Cindy glanced at Steven. "I didn't think it concerned you."

"It didn't concern me? I ought to paddle your backside, young lady."

"I wouldn't feel it if you did."

"Oh, I can make it hurt…believe you me."

"Dad…" she started, but Steven held up his hand and shook his head.

"We'll discuss this after dinner tonight. End of subject. Now, let's get back to some serious shooting."

Cindy slipped a pair of safety glasses on before aiming the 9mm semi-automatic pistol. She began pulling the trigger and quickly emptied the magazine.

Steven pulled a cable to retrieve the man-sized target, and held it up to the sunlight to study the results. He nodded his approval after a few seconds and passed the target to Cindy and Peter. The target had seven holes in a close pattern where a man's heart should be.

"Pretty nice shooting, Lieutenant Quintero," Steven said. "I'd say it was a lucky day for the al Qaeda when you got wounded and sent home."

Cindy finished reloading the magazine and snapped it back into the pistol.

"I think about that every night. I can't help feeling like I've somehow let my battle buddies down."

She aimed the pistol at a fresh target.

"I'd give my eye teeth for a chance to go back over there."

She pulled the trigger and quickly emptied the second magazine, then waited as Peter emptied an identical 9mm. They both turned to watch as Steven fired a much older and louder .44 caliber black powder pistol.

Chapter 30

Cynthia sat in her wheelchair staring up at Doctor Hastings as he viewed her chart. Edith dragged a chair close and sat to one side, waiting for the doctor to say something. There were two nurses on the opposite side of the large therapy room working with other patients.

"Well," Doctor Hastings said with a sigh. "These don't tell us a whole lot, but I saw you standing at the funeral on the news, so we know that's possible. How long do you think you were on your feet?"

"I honestly don't know," Cindy said with a shrug. "It was a spur of the moment thing. How come you weren't at the funeral? You knew Gary."

"I had an emergency. A sixteen-year-old decided to wreck his motorcycle."

"Oh, no!" Edith said. "Is he alright?"

"He'll live, but he was wearing sandals instead of boots, so he'll be missing part of one foot for the rest of his life. Now," he looked at Edith, "how long do you think she was standing?"

"She was on her feet two, maybe three minutes. It wasn't long, but longer than I thought she could."

"Two or three minutes is a long time."

Doctor Hastings grabbed a rolling stool and sat close to Cindy's chair. He took one of her ankles and flexed her foot and leg as he talked.

"We're going to get you on your feet in a minute, but not that long. We're going to believe you were able to stand that long because of your emotional attachment to Gary."

He lowered the leg he had been working on and repeated the exercise with her other leg.

"Another thing I'm sure helped you stand was the exercise routine Pete has you doing. You're in excellent shape."

He lowered her leg and stood.

"Okay, time to get started."

He rolled the stool aside and positioned a walker in front of her.

"Okay, Edith, I want you to stand on Cindy's right side and help her stand when I give the order. And Cindy, I want you to hold onto the walker. Easy now! Very slowly."

They helped her to her feet as she gripped the walker with white knuckles, then immediately tried to move forward.

"Whoa, hold on there, cowgirl," Randy said as he shook his head and laughed.

"Okay, easy. Mrs. Fowler, help her back into the chair."

"No! I wanna walk. Come on, Randy. I'm tired of sitting in that chair and making people wait on me."

"Not until you learn to listen. I don't want you getting hurt."

Cindy sat back in the chair with a scowl on her face.

"Now, be real honest," Randy said. "How did being on your feet feel?"

"It felt kind of funny. I knew I was standing, and I could feel some pressure on my legs, but I couldn't feel a lot."

"No pain?"

"Huh-uh." Cindy shook her head.

"You're sure? Honest?"

"None."

"Well," Doctor Hastings said with a smile. He took a deep breath and let it out slowly before glancing between Edith and Cynthia.

"I'm still not promising anything, but I'm pretty sure we'll get you back on your feet. You might have to use a walker, and maybe a back brace, but at least you'll be able to stand, maybe even walk, if you do what I say."

He grabbed his smart phone and started punching

buttons.

"I want you and Edith to practice standing three or four times a day, just a minute at a time."

He tossed Edith a cloth belt.

"Make sure you've got that belt fairly snug around her waist, and hold on in case she falls."

He turned to Cynthia.

"Don't try it without someone to help you. I don't want you falling and ruining everything we've accomplished so far."

He turned back to Edith.

"Buy a heavy-duty walker with some heft to it. Knowing her," he motioned toward Cindy, "she'll ignore everything I just said."

"Just say what I want and we'll get along fine," Cindy said with a laugh.

"The trouble is, saying what you want to hear could do some irreparable damage. If you try to do things to soon," he got fairly close to Cindy's face, "since you don't have feeling in your legs, you could trip and fall, or break a few bones; or, like an elderly gentleman just the other day—he fell and banged his head and died."

"Now," He sat on the stool and grinned, "Dr. Mills' report said part of your problem might be psychosomatic."

"She thinks I'm nuts?" A deep crease appeared between her eyes."

"No, you're not crazy. You really did get shot and you have some extensive nerve damage. What she's saying is there's a good chance you don't believe you *can* walk or deserve to walk. We're going to be working on that too."

He turned toward Edith and grinned. "I know it might be a real sacrifice, but she needs to continue seeing Deborah Mills for therapy, at least for a while."

"Steve and I are working on that right now."

"Good." Randy smiled at her for a few seconds.

"What?" Cindy said.

"Are you ready to try a few steps?"

"Say when." Cindy reached for the walker.

Chapter 31

"She thinks I'm crazy," Cindy said with a nervous giggle.

"Mmm, not really," Peter said as he wove Cindy's chair through the crowd toward the flag-draped stage and podium. "Psychosomatic problems are very real. Just as real as an automobile accident, or in your case, a gunshot wound."

He stopped her chair and allowed several children to dash across their path. They were being followed closely by Peter's parents who bumped into him as he stopped.

"According to her it's still inside my head, and that means I'm crazy."

"It sometimes manifests itself physically," Peter said thoughtfully. "If you don't believe me, take a look at mom's shiner. Besides," he stopped the chair in front of the stage, "we're all crazy to one degree or the other.

"I wanted to be a doctor, which means I never sleep or take care of myself. You wanted to be a Marine and go to war, which means you could and did get shot. Now, Curtis," Peter motioned toward Curt arguing with a young man about something to do with the staging, "wanted to become a politician. How crazy is that?"

Cindy didn't answer, as Curtis only glanced at her briefly while he gave the young man a stern talking-to in front of several people.

"No, I don't want to hear any excuses, Chuck. Every time I click the microphone on, I get feedback inside my earpiece."

"It's not my fault," the young man said. "I adjusted the

gain correctly, but every time you or Liz move something on stage, that changes everything. I caught her messing with the sound board just a minute ago."

"I don't care who causes what, or what it takes. I just want it fixed. Okay?"

Curtis turned his back on the young man before he could answer. He paused and took a deep breath before rushing toward Cindy with a big smile and giving her a quick kiss, then he shook the Fowler's hands.

"That was a little harsh, wasn't it?" Steven asked.

"What was?" Curt said.

"Degrading that fella in front of everyone."

Curt laughed and waved his hand as if he were shooing a fly.

"Oh, that. Charlie Hough is supposed to be one of the best sound men in Modesto. That's why Elizabeth hired him. But he's turned out to be a real idiot as far as I'm concerned. He can't get anything right. I'd replace him, but this thing starts in a few minutes. Speaking of which..." He checked his watch and started to turn away, but Edith caught his arm.

"Cindy has something to show you, Curt. I think it will make you happy."

Peter helped Cynthia to her feet, where she stood about fifteen seconds without any help. Then, Peter helped her sit back in the chair. Several teenage girls were gathered at the edge of the crowd watching them. One of the girls said something that made the others excited.

"Well, what do you think?" Cynthia asked.

Curtis was busy scanning the crowd, like he was trying to find someone in particular.

"Curt?" Cindy raised her voice.

"Mmm, yeah?" he said.

"I asked what you thought about me standing."

"Yeah, sure, that's great. Keep it up."

His expression suddenly changed as if he had found who he was searching for. He gave a brief wave before turning to kiss Cynthia on the forehead.

"Hey, I've got to catch Liz before this thing starts."

"Well," Edith heaved a big sigh, "that was sure telling."

Peter squatted on his heels to stare at Cynthia. She looked both crushed and perplexed.

"Hey, I'm sure he had a good reason for rushing off like that. You'll get to see him after the speech."

"Yeah," Cindy said. "You're probably right."

The teenage girls gathered at Cynthia's chair, grinning. "Excuse me," one of them said. "You're Lieutenant Quentero, aren't you?"

"Yes," Cindy said with a nod. "Yes I am."

She elbowed the one next to her. "See? I told you."

She turned back to Cindy. "Oh, gosh, you're one of my heroes! Would you please sign my program?"

Cynthia smiled and took the program. "Certainly, I'd be happy to sign your program. She searched for a ballpoint pen for a few seconds before Peter handed her one.

After she had finished signing the program, the other girls held theirs out for her signature. In a matter of seconds, a small crowd had gathered, all wanting Cynthia's signature or picture. Raymond Chandler appeared out of the crowd and joined Steven Fowler. He grinned and motioned toward Cynthia.

"Well, she's gotten pretty popular lately."

"She was already popular enough for my taste," Steven said. "After returning from Afghanistan, it was hard to take her anywhere without total strangers wanting to talk to her. Now, with Curt using her in his campaign…well, you can see for yourself."

Raymond chuckled.

"By the way," Steven said. "How come you're not running Curt's campaign anymore?"

Raymond cocked his head with a shrug.

"He decided he'd rather listen to Elizabeth Sparks than me. He kept complaining that he was behind in the polls. We were, but we were starting to climb, and still had plenty of time to pull ahead. We were set to win by sticking with the issues, but that wasn't good enough. He wanted the sensational. I'd warned him not to drag Cindy in, or I'd quit. I don't believe in using people like that."

"Like how?" Steven scrunched his brow.

"Nothing. I've said too much already," Raymond said. He swatted Steven on the shoulder. "Take it easy. I'll see you around, Steve."

Steven watched Raymond disappear into the crowd before turning back to watch Cynthia sign autographs and pose for photographs.

Be careful, baby. There's a skunk in the woodpile, and he's starting to stink the place up.

******

Peter stood at the edge of the crowd watching as the limousine driver helped Cynthia into the back seat next to Curtis. He had just endured forty-five minutes of listening to Curtis promise change after change to how state politics should be run, half of which he was sure Curtis never meant to fulfill.

Cynthia leaned forward to wave toward Edith and call out. "Bye. I'll be home late, so don't wait up."

"We'll leave a couple of lights on for you, dear," Edith yelled and waved back. "Be careful."

The driver closed the door and Curtis rolled the window down. "I'll take care of her, Mrs. Fowler. I promise."

Peter watched as the limousine disappeared down the street before turning to kiss his mother on the top of the head.

"I've got to make my rounds at the hospital. I'll give you a call in a day or two."

"Okay, dear." She stood on her tip-toes to kiss his cheek.

Peter shoved both hands into his jeans pockets as he ambled toward his truck. He sat in the driver's seat and turned to stare out the window with the corners of his mouth turned downward before starting the engine. Somehow, he felt like he needed to take a long, hot shower.

Chapter 32

Peter rose before daybreak and drove to the ranch, stopping at a Quick Stop for coffee on the way. He saddled his favorite horse, Buster, and galloped past the corral as the first rays of the sun peeked over the tops of the chinaberry trees. He rode past the herd of grazing cattle, to which he only gave a cursory glance, and stopped by a decaying log about a half a mile from the ranch house. He dismounted and sat on the log as he opened his copy of the New Testament and bowed his head.

"God, this hurts so much I can't stand it. You have to help me give her up. You know Cindy and I have known each other for most of our lives, and you also know that I've loved her every minute. But if you want her to be with Curt, I'll back away. I'll give her to him, but you'll have to help me, because honestly, all I feel like doing his smashing his pretty face. I'm sorry, but that's how I feel."

He checked his watch later as he rode back toward the ranch house, and was surprised to find he'd been praying and reading his New Testament for most of an hour. He was also surprised to find he didn't feel holy or closer to God. The only thing he was confident about was the fact that no matter what Cindy decided to do, God would give him the grace to accept the outcome.

Chapter 33

Edith placed several dirty plates into the dishwasher and turned it on. She grabbed a frying pan from the stove and placed it in the sink to wash as Cynthia entered the kitchen.

"Good morning, sleepyhead. Did you have a good time last night?"

"Yeah, I guess so," Cynthia said as she wheeled the chair to retrieve a coffee mug from a cup rack on the counter.

"Here," Edith said as she reached for the cup, "let me get that. I've got your breakfast staying warm in the oven."

Cynthia parked her chair at the table while Edith poured the coffee. Edith slid the mug in front of Cynthia, then pulled a foil-covered plate from the oven and placed it on the table.

"You don't sound too convincing. What happened? I thought he was taking you to dinner."

Cynthia took a sip of coffee and closed her eyes as she savored the flavor.

"He did. We went to a nice restaurant and he ordered steaks. I told him I'd already eaten, but he insisted. He said he was going to take care of his girl, so I'd better get used to it."

She snickered and took another sip of coffee.

"I told him I honestly didn't know I was his girl, because he'd never let me know where our relationship was headed. I mean, he said he loved me on stage that night, but I haven't heard him say that to me personally, ever. It would be nice to know how he really feels about us being together."

Edith peeled the foil from the plate and slid it in front of Cynthia. Cynthia stared at the sausage, scrambled eggs and fried potatoes.

"That looks good. Thank you, Mom."

Edith pulled a smaller plate of biscuits from the oven and slid them onto the table.

"Better eat while it's hot. Then what happened? What did he have to say after you told him you didn't know you were his girl?"

Cynthia buttered a biscuit and took a bite.

"He just laughed and kissed my cheek, then posed for another picture with his cheek pressed against mine."

She took a bite of sausage, savoring the flavor.

"That is *so* good. A whole lot better than the steak last night."

Edith poured herself a mug of coffee and sat at the table to study Cynthia.

"Why? What was wrong with it?"

"The steak?"

Edith nodded as she sipped her coffee.

"Nothing. It just didn't have much flavor. This has a little bite."

She took another bite of sausage and grinned. "I guess I'm a little more Mexican that I thought."

"We're all something," Edith said. "I like spicy food too." She took another sip of coffee. "So, tell me about the rest of your evening.

Cynthia snickered over a mouthful of scrambled eggs.

"I just did. There's not much to tell. I sat twiddling my thumbs, while Curt and Elizabeth spent the evening shaking hands and going to every table in the restaurant. Then they brought me home."

Edith crinkled her brow.

"That's it?"

Cindy swallowed another forkful of scrambled eggs.

"Oh, every once in a while, someone would want to take my picture, or ask for an autograph. But yeah," she nodded, "that's about it."

Edith heaved a deep sigh and took another sip from her mug.

"He's led a lot of people to believe you two are eventually going to get married. Especially since he's stated more than once publicly that he's in love with you. What are you going to say if he does ask you to marry him?"

Cynthia stared at Edith with a half a biscuit and a knife with butter in her hands.

"I don't know. I've always had a crush on him, but I haven't allowed myself to think about it."

"You'd better," Edith said, arching her eyebrows. "If you marry him, you can believe you'll have many more nights like last night. It's the nature of the political beast."

Cynthia finished buttering her biscuit and gave Edith a crooked smile.

"You certainly have a way of ruining a perfectly good breakfast."

She stared at Edith across the table, still holding the knife and biscuit in her hands.

"What should I do? I mean, I don't want to be treated that way the rest of my life. What do you think I should do? Tell him no?"

Edith laughed as she got up from the table and took her cup to the sink.

"I can't tell you that, honey. Curtis hasn't said he's in love with me, and we're not dating. That's something you'll have to answer for yourself. I'll pray that you make the right decision, but I'd advise you to pray about it yourself. Speaking of which, I haven't seen you studying your Bible and praying like you used to. What happened?"

"To tell the truth, God and me aren't exactly on speaking terms, since He allowed this to happen." Cindy patted the arm of her wheelchair.

Edith heaved a big sigh.

"I know how you must feel, but…"

"No you don't," Cindy said, cutting her off. "You can walk and drive a car and go places. You don't need someone to help you go to the bathroom."

She placed a hand on Cynthia's arm.

"That's true, I don't know how you feel. But there's nothing worse for a young woman than to marry the wrong man, for whatever reason. They'll become miserable and bitter the rest of their lives. You need to talk to God about you and Curt."

Edith walked to the sink and paused to look back.

"You were never happier than when you prayed and carried your Bible around, teaching others about Jesus. I miss that old Cindy."

She began scrubbing the frying pan. "God's got a plan for you, Cindy. But you'll never find it by pushing Him away.

Chapter 34

It was well past eleven and sleep was nowhere in sight. Cynthia sat in bed, propped upright by several pillows. She had her Bible opened in her lap, but it was a small photograph of Peter and her she found tucked inside the Bible that held her interest. Those were happy times. They were inseparable. Her eyes watered and a tear spilled over to land on the picture. She sniffed and wiped the tear away with her pajama sleeve.

She could remember the day Edith took the picture. They had gone on a picnic near the south paddock while the spring flowers were in full bloom. Edith had Becky toddling around in diapers at the time and had just discovered she was pregnant with Seth, But Cindy had begged to see the flowers, so Edith packed sandwiches, chips and apple juice. Peter, Bobby and Cindy had run races and had a contest on who could find a four-leafed clover.

She covered her mouth with one hand and shut her eyes.

"Oh God ... I don't know what to do. Please help me. Please, God, help me to know what to do."

Chapter 35

"Aagh!" Zoe screamed and pounded the steering wheel with her fists. Her car had simply quit running as she turned onto McHenry Avenue. She allowed it to coast into the Denny's parking lot, where she tried starting it again. She finally gave up after draining the battery. Throwing the transmission into neutral, she leaned her 115 pound body against the trunk. Her legs and stomach muscles burned as the clunker slowly inched itself forward.

Satisfied she wasn't blocking anybody from entering or leaving Denny's, she grabbed several plastic grocery bags filled with her things and kicked the car door closed before crossing McHenry Avenue. Her cellphone said it was 12:30 a.m. She glanced around at the neon-lit avenue as she walked briskly north, staying in the center of the sidewalk. Some grizzled old man asked if she had any loose change, so she dug into the pocket of her faded jeans and gave him her last fifty cents.

"God bless you, young lady," he said as she continued her march.

Yeah, I'm sure. I'm real close to having to sleep next to you on the street, old man.

She guessed it might've been close to three miles to Fred's house, and she wasn't sure he would be home, or even if he would take her in, but she had nowhere else to go. She checked her phone again as she stepped up on Fred's front porch and rang the doorbell. It was 1:35 in the morning. She waited a few seconds before ringing again. She rang a third time before sliding down the door frame to sit on the porch as a flood of tears spilled over.

Fred opened the door and stared at her with bleary eyes. "Zoe! What are you doing here?" He repeated the question as she sat there sobbing. He tried to open the screen door, but her body was blocking the door.

"Zoe? Scoot over and I'll let you in." The crying didn't stop so Fred sat on the floor next to the door until she quit.

"Scoot over. I can't open the door with you there."

She wiped her nose against her sleeve as she crawled away from the screen door. Fred helped her to her feet and ushered her to the sofa. He tossed her a box of tissues before moving the plastic bags inside and locking the door.

"Stay there and relax. I'll get you something to drink." She could hear the microwave hum then ding seconds later. Fred came back into the living room with a cup of hot chocolate.

"Go ahead and drink it. It'll help calm you," he said as she stared at the mug.

"I'm vegan, remember? This has milk in it."

"Yes, but this is different. It will do you good. Go ahead."

Zoe sipped the warm liquid and raised her eyebrows.

"It does taste good."

"I told you. You can always trust me, Zoe. I won't lie or hurt you."

He moved the coffee table a few inches so he could sit on an ottoman facing her. He leaned over and unlaced her tennis shoes. "Want to tell me what's going on?"

"My feet are sweaty and probably stink."

"Maybe, but that's not answering my question. What happened?"

"Mom's boyfriend can't keep his hands to himself. He snuck into my bedroom while I was sleeping and started feeling me up. I woke up and slapped his face and got this in return." She turned her head to show him a black eye.

Fred removed her socks and examined her swollen feet.

"You've got some blisters. Your shoes must not fit you good." He rose from the footstool and leaned to kiss her eye tenderly. "He hit you hard enough to break the skin. I'll be right back."

He disappeared into the bathroom and returned with a tube of antibiotic salve and a bottle of skin lotion. He dabbed a little salve on her eye, then began massaging her feet with the lotion. "Where is your car?"

"In the Denny's parking lot. The stupid thing died and wouldn't start. She finished her chocolate and leaned her head back and closed her eyes. "Mmm, that feels good, even if my feet are stinky."

"You can take a shower in the morning. Right now, we need to think about what's going to happen tomorrow."

"I was going to sleep in the car, but I wouldn't get much sleep in Denny's parking lot. Can I spend the night here?"

"Yes. I don't want you sleeping in the car, period. It's too dangerous. And I don't want you going back home if your mom's boyfriend is going to try molesting you. Come here." Fred held out his hand to help her to her feet.

"Ow!" she said, limping as she followed.

"I told you," he said with a chuckle. He opened the door to the guest room and studied her for a few seconds. "Here's your room for as long as you want. All I ask is that you keep it clean and don't have a bunch of friends over while I'm gone. I have a lot of expensive equipment here. Is that a deal?"

"I can sleep in your bed, if you want me to."

Fred raised his eyebrows and slowly shook his head. "I would like that very much, except we've both been hurt and have too much baggage."

Her eyes misted as she squeezed his hand. "Who hurt you?"

"I was engaged to be married. The day before the wedding I caught her in bed with my best man. I didn't feel like sharing her that way. Now, I'm kind of like you. I don't trust people too easily."

"Stupid..." Zoe cursed mildly as she hugged him. "I wouldn't ever do that to you, Fred."

"I know you wouldn't Zoe. But, I don't think God would like us fornicating with each other."

"You believe all that God stuff?"

"Yeah, I do," he said with a nod. "Don't you?"

"No. I've prayed most of my life and look what it's gotten me. I'm not even sure there is a God."

"Well, let's try it my way first before throwing God out the window, okay?" He reached down and scooped her in his arms and deposited her on the bed.

"You know where everything is, so make yourself at home. I'll get your bags. Oh," he added at the doorway. "I'll need the keys to your car. I'll call a friend of mine who knows something about cars to look at it."

"Sure." Zoe dug the keys from her pocket and tossed them to him. "I hope it's a different friend."

"Pardon?"

"Your friend. I hope he's not the one you found with your fiancé."

"No," Fred said with a chuckle. "He's a totally different guy."

******

Zoe woke late with the smell of coffee and the sound of a lawnmower next door. "Ow! Ow!" she cried as she limped toward the bathroom. Every part of her body hurt, but mostly her feet. She opted for a long hot bath, hoping it would ease some of the muscle pain. After soaking for a half an hour, her stomach started growling. Realizing she hadn't eaten anything since breakfast the previous day, she rummaged around in the refrigerator.

"Eggs, a pound of bacon, milk, bread, butter. Typical man of the house."

Finding a box of Cheerios in the cupboard, she opted for a bowl of cereal with milk, even though it wasn't on her diet, and a cup of black coffee. She found a folded piece of paper with *Zoe* written on the outside lying by the coffee pot.

Well, that didn't take long. She pushed the bowl of cereal away and unfolded the paper. *He musta decided I was going be too much trouble.*

Her eyes watered as she read the note:

Zoe. I'm sorry I don't have much that you like to eat inside this house. We'll go shopping when I get home and load up. I think we also need to get you a decent pair of shoes. I'd recommend calling in sick today. Your feet need to take a day off.

Her chin trembled as she pulled the bowl and mug back in front of her. She took a couple of bites but had trouble swallowing. Finally, she burst into tears.

Oh, God, please don't let him get tired of me. Help me. I don't want to lose him also. He's the nicest guy I know. Please make him like me.

Zoe had never considered herself a good judge of character. She was maybe the worst, considering she'd lost every boyfriend she had, and most of them fairly quickly. But for some reason, Fred Nunez seemed different than the rest. She couldn't quite put her thumb on it, but her gut told her it was true. Well, the simple fact that he didn't want her to disrobe and crawl into his bed made him different.

She spent the afternoon rummaging through photo albums and a collection of CDs. Most of the CDs turned out to be vintage heavy metal hits. She had never heard of most of the bands, so she popped a couple into the player. She did her laundry listening to the sound of *Metallica*.

******

Fred parked in the driveway, knowing he would be leaving fairly quickly to take Zoe shopping. Shopping was never his favorite thing to do, but tonight he welcomed the distraction. Filming a crash on Highway 99 at Beckworth Road left him feeling flat. A drunken driver had pulled onto the highway going the wrong way and hit a car head-on, killing the entire family, including a ten-month old child. He found himself wishing he had been filming one of Curt's campaign speeches, which didn't rate very high either.

He opened the door to be assaulted by *Led Zeppelin* with the aroma of coffee and bacon.

"I didn't know what you liked, so I fixed you breakfast for dinner. I hope that's alright," Zoe said as she draped her arms around his neck. She kissed him on the lips and smiled.

"Yeah, that's great, but what about you? What are you going to eat?"

"I can find something when we go to the store. This is for you being so kind and nice and letting me stay here last night." She pulled a chair away from the table. "Sit down while I fry your eggs."

Fred sipped his coffee while watching her at the stove. It was like watching a rock opera. She was standing in front of the stove in bare feet, with her spiked orange hair and tattoos, frying eggs and swaying to the music. He grinned as he sipped his coffee.

"Do you like Zeppelin?"

"I'd never heard them before today," she said. "But yeah. I do like them."

She slid a plate in front of him that contained three slices of bacon, two eggs, toast and fried potatoes. She then sat opposite him with one piece of bacon between her fingers and smiled before taking a bite.

Fred raised his eyebrows. "I didn't know vegans ate bacon."

Zoe held a finger to her lips. "Shhhh, they don't. But this smelled so good that...well...I'm cheating."

Fred smiled as he placed a forkful of potatoes into his mouth.

Who needs T.V.? She's entertainment enough. Yeah, I could get used to this real quick.

Chapter 36

Peter stopped to wipe sweat from his face. He had chosen to spend his day off helping his father buck hay inside the hay barn in preparation for winter. His father had enlisted Seth and Miguel to help and, as usual, they wanted to turn the project into some sort of contest. Today's contest was the old guys versus the young guys. Not that Peter considered himself to be "old" by any means. But in Seth's mind, anyone past twenty-five years was ancient.

"So, what are you going to do? Sit back and let her marry that knot-head?" Steven passed another bale to Peter, who stacked it and turned for another.

"What are you talking about? Let who marry who?"

Steven handed him another bale with a growl.

"You know who I'm talking about. Cindy and that Curt character."

Peter wiped his brow on his shirt sleeve and took another bale from his father.

"You know, I didn't come out here on my day off to listen to one of your lectures about me and Cindy."

Steven grabbed another bale and shook his head.

"You are going to let her marry him, aren't you?"

"I can't tell her what to do. If she wants to marry him, that's her business. I don't have any ties on her. Come on, Give me another bale. They're ahead."

Steven passed another bale and took a sip of water from a bottle.

"So, let 'em. They're younger, and I'm paying their salaries. Let 'em earn it." He raised his voice. "Take a break, boys."

Steven opened a cooler and pitched a bottle of water to each person. Seth and Miguel stopped working and sat on bales to drink their water. Steven took a long swig and pointed the bottle at Peter with a stern look.

"If you don't think that girl listens to you, you're dumber'n dirt. She's always followed you like a lost puppy. Ain't that right, boys?"

Seth and Miguel laughed as Peter glared at his father.

"That she does," Miguel said. "That's why she joined the Marines." He motioned toward Peter with his half-empty bottle. "She thought it would make you happy."

"Well, yeah," Peter said. "We've always been friends, but never romantic. We're like brother and sister."

"No," Seth said, shaking his head. "Bobby was like our brother. Cindy worships the ground you walk on. She wore jeans, boots and a cowboy hat before it became popular. Then, when you started talking about joining up and going off to war, she joined the Marines. She did it because you said you were going to, only you changed your mind and didn't join."

Peter capped his bottle with disgust and hauled another bale by himself.

"You're all nuts! And this hay isn't going to stack itself."

The others capped their bottles and went back to work.

"Here," Steven said. "You pass them up to me. I'm tired of lifting them over my head to you."

Peter passed several bales to his father before Steven reached for one and quickly released it. The bale hit Peter in the stomach as he turned, knocking him to a sitting position.

"Hey! That could hurt someone," Peter yelled.

"Not half as bad as what you're doing to that poor girl."

Peter grabbed the bale and passed it back to his father.

"I'm doing to her? What exactly am I doing to her? She's in love with Curt. You want me to break them apart?"

Steven stacked the bale and reached for another.

"Now, that's the best idea I've heard coming from you

in a month."

Peter stopped with a bale in his hands.

"Well, what am I supposed to do, Pop? She told me she had had a crush on him since we were all in high school."

Steven wiped the sweat from his face.

"Have you ever told her you're in love with her?"

Peter glanced silently at the others.

"You might as well," Steven said. "We all know you are. We've known it all along. But I'll bet you've never told her, have you?"

Peter remained silent.

"Aggh…" Steven motioned toward Peter like he was shooing a fly. "I'll never understand you, boy. You'll patch someone who's been in a wreck back together or slice them wide open and fix what's wrong, but you're afraid to tell Cindy you're in love with her."

He grabbed another bale and stacked it by himself.

"There's no use in talking to you. You're gonna stand by and let her ruin both of your lives." He grabbed another bale and lifted it in place.

"Come on, boys. Let's finish this before we run out of daylight."

Chapter 37

Cynthia's mouth felt as dry as a handful of sand. "Excuse me." She took time to survey the crowded auditorium as she took a sip of water from a plastic cup. She had turned Curtis down when he first asked her to give a speech.

"You've got to be kidding. I don't give speeches, Curt. I never have."

"That's not true. I used to watch you in the lunch room every day, talking to that bunch of girls back in high school."

"I wasn't giving speeches back then. We were studying the Bible. Besides, no one's interested in listening to me talk, even if I *had* something to say…which I don't."

"Just say what's on your heart. Tell the audience what you've been dying to say to the American people since you've returned home." That was exactly what she had done. After a week of constant badgering, she had relented and said yes. Now, she was down to her last few sentences, and happy to be finished.

"And, because of the money shortage and red tape, many of our wounded veterans are finding it difficult to get the care they need, especially the females. No veteran … absolutely not one … should ever be homeless and sleeping on the street."

She paused to smile at the audience.

"Thank you for being kind and listening."

Curtis stepped forward and waited for the applause to die down.

"Thank you, Cindy. Now, we have just enough time for one or two quick questions.

Cynthia could see Elizabeth Sparks to the right of the

stage as she pointed toward a young man holding a microphone.

"You on the third row," Curtis said. "James, isn't it?"

"Yes; James Adams from CBS Evening News." He paused to clear this throat. "Miss Quentero, thank you for a very informative speech. I do have one question I hope you can shed some light on. The wars in the Middle East seem to have gotten muddled, especially the one in Afghanistan. Could you please identify the problems our soldiers are facing, and what can be done to cure them?"

Cindy sat thoughtfully for a few seconds before giving a crooked grin.

"If we had a week to discuss the issue, maybe. But I don't know that I'm qualified, or know all the problems." They waited for the laughter to subside.

"Well, please try," James said.

Cindy grew solemn and stared at the ceiling for a few seconds.

"War changes people. The change begins when you hear the first shot or explosion, and have to return fire. Watching an enemy fall because you have shot him changes something inside you. Or, when you hold a friend in your arms while he dies, it will make you different."

She stared at her upturned palms, and heaved a deep sob as she envisioned Captain Miller's blood covering her uniform.

"It would be next to impossible to understand, unless you have been there, but I'll try."

She sniffed and took the box of tissues Curtis handed her, trying to compose herself.

"The problem as I see it—well, where do we begin? We spend billions of dollars each year, training and equipping the best military in the history of the world then allow politicians, many who have never worn a uniform or held a gun, to conduct the war from their comfortable chairs in their air conditioned offices for political reasons."

The audience erupted into applause as they rose to their feet. She waited until the ovation had quieted before continuing.

"Congress and the president need to maintain the right to declare war, but if they are going to send men and women into harm's way, they should allow them to fight as they are trained. The war would end quicker, at less cost, and there would be fewer casualties on both sides."

Again, there was a roar of applause as the audience remained standing.

Curtis stepped forward and took a minute to silence the audience.

"Sadly, we have run out of time for more questions. I would like to end this evening with giving Lieutenant Quentero a little gift of appreciation."

He handed Cindy a large envelope.

"What's this?"

"Open it."

Cindy pulled a stack of papers from the envelope and stared at them.

"It is an application for a grant to help with your rehabilitation center. It won't pay for the entire center, but it will certainly give you a good start." He paused to smile at her. "It's all been filled out. All you have to do is sign the last page."

Cindy fumbled with the papers, trying to stuff them back into the envelope.

"Thank you. I ... don't know what to say."

Curtis knelt beside her on stage and slipped an arm around her shoulders.

"You don't have to say anything. You and the other men and women in the armed forces deserve much more than what's inside that application."

They were interrupted by another round of applause.

"I really wish it could be more," he said as he pulled a ring box from his coat pocket, opened it and handed her the ring. "Especially for the woman I love."

At this point, the crowd went crazy with applause and whistles. Cindy squinted her eyes as cameras flashed all over the auditorium. She sat transfixed, staring at the ring.

Elizabeth Sparks grinned as she pumped her fist into the air. "Yes! Yes! That did it!" she said under her breath.

"Wow!" Cindy said. "I...never expected anything like this, 'Curt. I...don't know what to say."

"Just say you'll think about it. In the meantime," Curtis took the ring and slipped it on her finger. "Just wear it. Perhaps you will enjoy the feel enough to say yes."

"Yes!" Cindy nodded briskly.

"What?"

"Yes, I will marry you." The audience went wild as Cindy grabbed Curt and kissed him.

Curtis waited until the audience had calmed and held Cindy's hand high for the audience to see the ring. "It does look pretty on her finger, doesn't it?"

The audience again roared with applause as cameras flashed. Peter was standing next to his father, but neither of them were applauding or cheering. Steven leaned close to Peter's ear and raised his voice.

"I told ya! Numbskull."

Chapter 38

Edith drove her Ford Expedition down the field road toward a large corral where Steven, Seth, Miguel and Peter were busy branding cattle. Edith guided the vehicle next to the pen and Cindy lowered her window as the two dogs, Jasper and Sally, barked and chased a young bull into the chute, where Steven locked the gate. Peter filled a syringe and gave the bull an injection as Seth dehorned the bull and Miguel applied the branding iron.

"Well, I guess it's settled then. You really are a horse doctor," Cindy said to Peter with a bright smile. The smile quickly faded as Peter just looked at her and refilled the syringe for the next bull.

Steven left the corral and leaned close to Cindy's opened window. "Where are you two off to?"

"To do some grocery shopping." Edith almost yelled to be heard over the barking dogs and bawling cattle. "You want anything special?"

"Mmm, some rocky road ice cream would be nice."

"Rocky road it is. Dinner's at six."

Edith put the SUV in gear and drove away. Steven entered the corral and glared at Peter as he locked the gate on the next calf that the dogs chased into the chute.

"How long are you gonna nurse that grudge against Cindy?"

"Just about as long as you keep sticking your nose where it doesn't belong," Peter snapped.

Steven left the gate and glared at Peter up close.

"When it concerns my family, it *is* my business. And

maybe you should stop back-talking your father."

They quickly finished and released the calf while the dogs chased another bull into the chute.

"What's eating him?" Miguel asked.

"He sat back and let that shifty-talking politician steal Cindy. That's what's eating at him."

"Nah," Miguel shook his head. "I don't think she'll marry that guy. Not Cindy."

Miguel applied the branding iron to the bawling calf.

"I wouldn't be too sure. Women are curious critters, and they're liable to do most anything if they feel unwanted." Steven released the steer and waited for the dogs to chase another into the chute. "And I'm afraid that's exactly what my knot-headed son is doing to her."

Chapter 39

It took three days for Peter to calm himself and make an attempt to talk to Cynthia and treat her civilly. He wasn't having much success at thinking kind thoughts toward Curtis, but he figured he could simply stay clear of him until God saw fit to give him an extra dose of grace. He stopped at Walmart and bought a new checker game and pasted on his best smile as he entered the ranch house.

"Where's Mom and Dad?" he asked, setting up the board.

"They said they had some errands to run in town." Cindy shrugged her shoulders. "That's all I know. Why? You need to see them for something?"

"No. I actually came to apologize to you."

"Really? What about?"

"For treating you rudely when you tried talking to me at the corral the other day. I was way out of line."

"Yes, you were," Cindy said as she rolled her chair up to the game table. "Apology accepted."

Peter finished setting up the board and grinned. "Ready to get clobbered?"

"Now, that's not gonna happen. I'll give you the first move."

They were on their third match with Cindy holding a two to one advantage when Peter broached the subject of the ring on Cindy's finger.

"So," he took her left hand and studied the ring. "At least he's not a cheapskate."

"No, it really is a nice ring. What made you think he

was cheap?"

"No reason," he said and he made his move. "King me."

Cindy crowned the piece and studied the board.

"I've always had the impression that Curt might be crass and down-right rude at times, but never cheap. Do you have a problem with me getting married?"

"No, I don't have a problem with you getting married."

"Good," she said as she jumped three of his checkers.

"Huh," Peter stared at the board. "I didn't see that coming."

"Obviously." Cindy folded her hands like she was praying and grinned at him. "You don't have a problem with me getting married. Then, what's the problem? Why have you been so angry with me?"

"It's just *who* you're going to marry. Why Curt?"

"Why not Curt?" The crease between her eyes grew deep. "He's popular, comes from a rich family, and he's not bad looking. Why not him?"

"Yeah, but Curt? You can do better than that, Cindy. A lot of guys would marry you."

"Really? He's the first guy that's shown any interest in me since Afghanistan."

She backed the wheelchair away from the game table.

"Take a good look at me, Pete. I'm almost thirty, stuck in this stupid chair, and I'll never get out. I don't have much choice, do I?"

She spun the chair and headed toward her room.

"That's not true," he yelled after her. "You're making progress every day, and a lot of guys love you. I love you!"

She jerked her bedroom door open and yelled back down the hall.

"Yeah, but brothers are supposed to love their sisters. That's what they do. And I'm sick and tired of everyone criticizing and telling me what to do. Just leave me alone!"

Cynthia banged her door closed, leaving him to stare at the empty hallway.

"Yeah, I guess we are supposed to love our sisters."

Peter grabbed his hat and stormed out the door and toward his truck.

Chapter 40

"She's been through a lot, Pete." Becky placed several rolls of surgical tape in the supply cabinet and shook her head. "None of us knows what she's really been through."

"True, but trying to deal with her mood swings hasn't been a picnic either. All I asked her was why she wanted to marry Curt. What was wrong with that?"

"Nothing...on the surface." She said as she counted surgical kits in a different drawer.

"What do you mean, *on the surface*? Either she knows why she's marrying him, or she doesn't know. How hard is that?"

Becky stopped restocking the cabinet and heaved a deep sigh.

"Look, you're my brother, so let me give you a piece of advice, okay?"

"Shoot," Peter said after a few seconds.

"In her mind, she doesn't have many options. Most of the people our age are already married, at least the ones we know. Cynthia was known for her athletic ability, so it didn't surprise me when she joined the Marines. Now, she's back home and crippled. In her mind, everything she knows and loves is gone."

"That's not true..."

"Please, let me finish. *I* may know that God has something great planned for her life, but she doesn't."

Becky returned to the drawer, and turned back toward Peter. "Let me ask you this. You don't like the idea of Cindy marrying Curt, and that's fine. But have you asked her to marry *you?*"

She stared at him a silent moment, then shook her head. "I didn't think so. Don't complain if you're not willing to step up to the plate and swing the bat."

Chapter 41

Cindy crouched behind a Humvee holding her M4 rifle. The sound of machine gun fire coming from the hillside was mingled with the rattling of bullets hitting the side of the vehicle. She carefully craned her neck for a glimpse over the hood, but ducked down quickly as a bullet hit the windshield dangerously close to her head.

Captain Miller was lying on his back in a pool of blood. She yelled "Medic! Medic! Captain Miller is down!" She leaned away from the Humvee to see, but there was no Medic in sight.

"Where are you? He's going to die waiting on you guys."

She peeped over the hood to see several Afghan rebels advancing toward her. She aimed her M4 at the nearest rebel and pulled the trigger, but the gun didn't work.

"No! No!"

She pulled the slide to inject a new round into the chamber and aimed the gun once more, but it still didn't fire.

"Work, you stupid thing! Work!"

She ejected the magazine and popped another into place and pulled the slide. Captain Miller's head suddenly became detached and rolled toward her boots as he said, "Help me, Lieutenant. Help me!"

"Oh! No, no, no!" She pressed her back against the Humvee.

The rebels were on top of her now, only a matter of yards away. Suddenly, the heads of all her battle-buddies came rolling toward her feet saying, "Help me, Lieutenant! Help us!"

Cindy bolted upright in her bed. "Oh, God, please help me! Oh, God!"

Edith opened the bedroom door and poked her head inside.

"Are you alright, honey?"

"Yeah, Mom," she said with a nod. "Just a bad dream."

"Want some company? I'll sit with you."

"No...I'm okay now. Really. Go back to bed."

Chapter 42

"I don't know what it means," Becky said with a chuckle. She was on the floor in front of Cindy, holding her legs down as Cindy did sit-ups.

"Don't they teach you nurses something about psychology?"

"Well, yeah, a little. But you're asking me to interpret a dream, and I'm not sure dreams mean a whole lot, especially mine. Come on, twenty more," she said as Cindy stopped doing sit-ups.

"You'd think differently if you had been in Afghanistan."

"I think you're probably correct. But you're talking about severe trauma, and that's a whole different subject. Okay, you can stop now," she said after Cindy had finished her sit-ups. "Let's roll you over on your stomach."

"It seemed so real," Cindy said as Becky helped her roll to her stomach.

"Mmm, maybe a little."

"I'm not making this up, Becky. I had sweat dripping from my body. I could even hear the crunch of their boots as they advanced on my Humvee."

"But you said everyone in your dream died, didn't you?"

"Yeah; well, sort of. What I said was, all their heads came off and rolled toward me. That's when I woke up."

"And what happened to their bodies?"

"What about their bodies?"

"People don't live without a head, Cindy. Did their

bodies just keel over and die?"

"No," Cindy said thoughtfully. "I remember seeing Jackson manning the machine gun on the back of the Humvee."

"Without a head?"

"Yeah...I guess so."

"I think you've just answered your question," Becky said, kneeling at Cindy's head on the floor. "It was just a dream—a nightmare that spooked you. Who knows why you dreamed it. Maybe you feel like you didn't do enough. Now, come on, we can talk as you do your push-ups. Give me twenty-five."

Without feeling or controlling her legs, the push-ups consisted of lifting the upper half of her body, while her legs lay limp on the floor.

"So, what are you driving at?" Cindy said between push-ups.

"Simply this. How many really died that night?"

"Three."

"There you go," Becky said.

"There I go what?"

"Like I said, your dream was simply that—a dream. I'm not sure it means anything. Everyone, including Captain Miller, kept their heads. Now, tell me the latest on Curt."

"Thanks for listening to me. I know I sound crazy sometimes," Cindy dropped to the floor laughing. "It seemed so real it was bothering me."

"You're quite welcome. I'll just add a fee to the end of my bill. Now, what's the latest on Curt? Mom mentioned something about a great big gala thing Curt's going to be doing at the Gallo Center. What's that all about?"

"Oh, help me sit up and I'll tell you."

Becky helped her roll over and lean back against the sofa then quickly handed her two ten-pound dumbbells.

"You can talk while you exercise."

"It takes place three days before the election. It's something Elizabeth Sparks came up with. She's hired a couple of local bands as a *thank you* to his supporters. She said it will seal the election for him."

"She seems to think of everything, doesn't she?"

"She tries. Are you going?"

"Are you going to speak?"

"I don't know," Cindy said as she lowered the dumbbells. "He might have me greet the crowd. He asked me to wear my dress uniform with the medals."

"I might go just to get a good picture of you on stage."

"Are you gonna vote for him?"

"Now, that is rather personal." Becky said with a grin.

"I don't know what everyone in this house has against Curt. It's like he ran over one of the dogs…or worse. What is it with you guys?"

"I can't speak for Seth or Mom and Dad, or especially Pete. But I got called in on our last election day, and never even got to the polls. So, I'm voting absentee this year, and I haven't made up my mind on a couple of things."

"Better hurry. You've only got five days."

"I know. I'm off tomorrow and I'll do it then."

Becky started packing the exercise equipment and paused to stare at her.

"I heard you were going to marry him. The last time I talked to you, you didn't act like you wanted to. Are you sure?"

"Well, about as sure as most couples are. He gave me the ring in front of all those people, and everyone was cheering. I got caught up in everything, and I wasn't going to embarrass him by saying no in front of all those people."

"So, you said yes. If you're not sure, why didn't you say anything?"

"How could I? Everyone was cheering. They wanted some sort of an answer."

Becky laughed and shook her head.

"What? What's so funny?"

"What's funny is you. You're a Marine, Cindy, and

you've faced some really mean people who were trying to kill you. And you're afraid to tell Curt if you really want to marry him or not? Here," She set the bag with the exercise equipment aside. "Let me help you up."

She wrapped her arms around Cindy's waist and lifted.

"Couch or chair?"

"Couch."

Becky positioned her onto the sofa and moved her chair within reach.

"By the way, congratulations on your last therapy visit. I read your chart and it said you walked halfway across the room and back."

"Yeah, using the walker and going really slow."

"But you still did it. That's a large room, Cindy. I'm proud of you." She gave Cindy a warm smile. "It also said you've got some feeling back. Is that true?"

"Yeah." Cindy gave her a slow nod. "It feels like both legs are asleep. It's more irritating than anything."

"Maybe, but the thing is, you've got some feeling back." Becky leaned to give her a quick hug. "I've really gotta run."

"What about Pete?" Cindy asked as Becky reached for the bag of equipment.

"What about Pete?"

"Why doesn't he like Curt? I've asked him, but he's never given a real answer, yet he's always ragging on me about him."

"Well, you really should ask him that question. My guess is he's jealous. Bye." She waved and opened the door. "I'll see you in a couple of days."

Cynthia sat staring at the wall not really seeing anything until the sound of Edith's SUV on the graveled driveway snapped her back to reality.

Chapter 43

Charlie Hough adjusted the small security camera to make sure it caught most of the room and made sure it was working. He stepped back to see if the camera was visible from the far side of the room. Satisfied that no one, especially Curtis Roberts, would notice such an item next to a shelf loaded with microphones and wires, he re-checked the area being videoed on his smart phone and grinned. Lastly, he placed a microphone near the camera and turned it on. He had just suffered his third tongue-lashing of the day from Curtis, and decided to bring it all to an end.

"It's payback time, Curt. You've run up quite a bill. Now, let's see how you like it."

******

Peter entered the set of double doors pushing Cynthia's chair, followed closely by Seth and his parents. Cynthia had dressed in her uniform at Curt's request, with her medals proudly displayed on her chest. Much to Peter's surprise, the large auditorium was filling fast. He mentally chastised himself for not believing Curtis Roberts could draw such a large crowd.

He glanced around the noisy crowd and spied Curtis having an animated conversation with Charlie Hough inside the sound booth at the rear of auditorium.

"Here, let me take that," Steven said as he grabbed Cynthia's wheel chair. "We won't have a place to sit, if we keep standing here."

"Yeah, sure," Peter said with a nod. "Curt said he had seats reserved on the front row, but Cindy's supposed to be on stage. Save me a place."

Peter slowly wove his way through the crowd toward the sound booth. He opened the door and stepped inside to find the conversation a heated one.

"And who opened the doors early? I didn't get the room until forty-five minutes ago," Charlie was saying. "Then, you propped the doors open, while I'm trying to run wires and adjust the mikes and video and do a sound check."

Curtis tapped a printed copy of his speech against his thigh and glared.

"I opened the doors because they asked me to. The crowd was causing congestion, and I'm not going to chance losing supporters because you want an empty room to work in."

"Well, don't expect everything to work exactly like you want, because I haven't had a chance to test anything."

Curtis clenched his jaw in anger as he pointed a finger at Charlie.

"It had better work. The election is in three days and this is the most important night of my life. You'd better not screw it up, or I'll see that you never work another political campaign...ever."

Curtis turned to see Peter standing quietly in the corner and smiled.

"Hey Peter. We're in for an exciting night. Is Cindy here?"

"Right up front with my parents."

"Great! Does she have her uniform on?"

"Yes," Peter said with a chuckle, "with all the medals."

"Good, good," Curtis said, clasping Peter's shoulder. He opened the door, and then turned toward Charlie.

"You've got twenty minutes before kickoff. Check everything and make sure it works."

Curtis closed the door and wove his way toward a

door located next to the stage, shaking hands on the way.

Peter shook his head with a snicker. "Well, he's a piece of work, isn't he?

"Yeah, a real prince. Its guys like him who turn *politics* into a four-letter word."

Charlie adjusted a volume control on the sound board and listened to his headset, then nodded.

"What was that all about, anyway?" Peter asked.

"I was supposed to have this room two hours before they opened the doors, to get everything set up. Two hours turned out to be forty-five minutes, because a meeting they had in here earlier ran over." He paused to look at Peter with a crooked grin. "Elizabeth forgot to book this room when she should have. The only reason they let her have it at all is because her daddy is on the board, so they squeezed her in between shows."

Charlie turned a knob and flipped a switch. An image of Elizabeth perched on the edge of a table swinging one leg appeared on the monitor inside the sound booth.

"Then Curtis props all the doors open, letting people in. Now, he's mad because things aren't working exactly like he wants."

Charlie glanced at Peter and snickered.

"He said I'm not going to work another campaign? I can play that game too. I've been working his campaign long enough to know where the skeletons are. He's not really what people think he is."

Charlie flipped a couple of switches and the speakers inside the auditorium were filled with Curtis' voice, as an image of him entering the room off stage flashed on the large monitors stationed around the auditorium.

"Wireless mikes and security cameras are great, aren't they? Whoever wired this booth patched the off-stage room to this board in order to communicate with whoever's waiting off-stage. It's a great idea."

He laughed and shook his head.

"I sort of forgot to tell Curt about it."

He took Peter by the arm and ushered him out of the sound booth, locking the door behind them.

"Might as well watch it on a large screen."

Peter stared as the image of Curtis slipping into Elizabeth's arms and kissing her was plastered on every monitor.

"That's been going on since she took over his campaign. All that stuff he told that soldier girl was a lie. See you around."

Charlie gave Peter's shoulder a friendly swat and hurried toward the exit. He tossed the keys into a trash can as he left the auditorium. Peter jerked up to stare at one of the monitors at the sound of Elizabeth's voice.

"What took you so long?"

"Oh, that idiot we hired to run the sound had everything screwed up. He was trying to blame me; said I opened the doors early."

Elizabeth gave him a quick kiss.

"What did he expect you to do? It takes time to fill a room this size."

The noise level inside the auditorium had lowered considerably. Peter glanced at the crowd to discover everyone was watching the monitors. He could see his father's head from where he stood outside the sound room. He had parked Cindy's chair on the front row of seats and was watching one of the monitors. Cindy was watching the same monitor.

"No, no, no!" Peter rushed through the crowd toward the door off stage and burst inside. He pulled the door closed with a bang as Curtis jerked free of an embrace in Elizabeth's arms.

"What do you think you're doing? He yelled in Curtis' face.

"No, the question is, *What do you think you're doing*? This room is supposed to be private."

"You should have locked the door," Elizabeth said as she checked her makeup in a compact mirror.

"I thought it was locked," Curtis said.

"You gave Cindy a ring," Peter yelled as he crossed the small room toward them. "You're supposed to be engaged to her. What's going on?"

Elizabeth laughed as she snapped the compact close. "What does it look like? I thought that was obvious."

"Come on, Pete. I might've given her a ring, but you don't really expect me to marry her, do you?"

Elizabeth broke into a fit of giggles. "Can you...can you honestly see Curt pushing a crippled Mexican down the halls of the Capitol Building?"

"Well, yeah," Peter said. "Since you gave her the ring in front of a thousand people, and said you loved her. I did expect you to marry her."

"It wouldn't be fair to either one of us, if I did, Pete. I'd be in meetings that I couldn't take her to, and I'd have to travel." He paused to look at Peter and heaved a deep sigh.

"Just ask yourself. If you were me, would you marry her, knowing she'll never walk again or be normal?"

Peter turned away, and then paused at the door.

"Yeah, a lot of guys would jump at the chance. She's a great girl."

He put his hand on the panic bar to open the door, and then paused to look over his shoulder once more.

"By the way, Charlie Hough said to tell you he quit."

"He what?" Curtis pulled completely away from Elizabeth. "He can't do that! The show's starting in five minutes."

"Well, he did and, before he left, he flipped switches and turned some dials, then locked the door. The camera and microphone inside this room is hot."

Elizabeth laughed loudly.

"Get real, Pete. We're too old to play games like that."

Someone pounded on the door and shook it, trying to get in.

"Okay," Peter said and let go of the panic bar. "See

for yourself."

The door flew open and the room was suddenly filled with camera flashes and voices as news men and women flooded the room, shoving microphones in Curtis and Elizabeth's faces. Peter pushed through the reporters and worked his way toward his father. People were leaving the auditorium in a mass exodus.

Curtis ignored the questions and muscled his way into the auditorium, yelling. "No! Wait! Everyone, please wait! There's been a huge mistake here. It was all a bad joke."

Curtis spied Cynthia, who was trying desperately to ignore a news woman, and get her wheelchair turned. Peter joined Steven and Edith, who were trying to clear a path for her.

Beads of moisture trickled down Curtis' brow as he rushed toward Cindy. "Cindy," he yelled, grabbing the back of Cindy's chair. "Cindy!"

He tried spinning her toward him as she pulled away. "Cindy, please! Just listen."

She jerked back on one of the wheels, breaking free of his hold.

"Leave me alone, Curt!"

"Please, Cindy. Please, just listen. It's not what it looks like."

"I don't care. Go away!"

She jerked off the engagement ring and threw it at his face. "Take your stupid ring and leave me alone!"

She tried once more to turn the chair, but he grabbed one of the armrests and held tight. A small army of reporters and cameramen had gathered and were happily recording the entire proceeding. Cindy caught a glimpse of the girl with orange hair standing on a row of chairs, manning a video camera.

"Please, Cindy. Just listen."

She locked her jaw tightly, twisting her upper body as Curtis gripped her shoulders.

Curtis moved in close to her face, pleading with her. "Just hold still and listen to me."

"Get out of my face!"

Cynthia thrust out her right hand, hitting his nose with the heel of her palm. The force of the blow knocked him backward to the floor. She sat a few seconds, staring at Curt lying on the floor, before spinning her chair and headed toward the exit amid cheers and applause from those still inside the building. Several newsmen followed her toward the exit while the rest focused on Curtis, who had now rolled over holding his nose as blood dripped between his fingers.

"Oh! I think she broke my nose!"

Elizabeth had exited the side room and stood looking on in shock, until Zoe swung her video camera her way. She quickly disappeared back inside the room, locking the door.

Curtis pulled a handkerchief from his pocket and covered his nose as he slowly crawled to his feet. He half-staggered toward the door off stage only to find it locked. He pounded on it with his fists and yelled.

"Liz, Liz! Come on, Liz. Open the door!"

******

"Was that exciting enough for you?" Fred asked as he joined Zoe. Almost everyone had followed Cindy's wheelchair outside, leaving a handful of reporters and staff inside. A janitor was busy trying to extract Curt's blood from the carpet. Nearly all the reporters were on their cell phones telling their agencies what had taken place.

"I got some great shots," Zoe bubbled as she bounced up and down.

"Any good video?"

"I locked onto Cindy the moment Curt started begging. I caught everything."

"Me too. Come on," Fred said, taking her arm. "Let's head to the studio and edit the film. They're gonna want to use this tonight."

Zoe hugged the cameras close to her body following on Fred's heels as he pushed through the doors.

An hour and a half later, Zoe uploaded her video to YouTube and sat back sipping her coffee. Her heart seemed to pick up speed as she watched the counter register hits on her video. By the time Fred had finished being interviewed by Rita Lorenzo on air the counter had passed three thousand hits and was picking up speed. It would be even faster after Rita had finished her broadcast. Zoe's only concern now was the possibility of crashing Fred's website. She had added a small message at the end, advertising the video as courtesy of *Fred & Zoe's Photography Studio*, with a website address. She was interested in seeing if that brought Fred any business.

Chapter 45

Cindy blinked back the pain and struggled to sit upright on the floor next to her bed. Her right cheek was bruised and swollen. The tissue she pressed against the wound came back with a small amount of blood, telling her it was scraped or cut. Her walker was tipped over, blocking the door. Her nightstand was lying on its side with the lamp base shattered, and the contents of the drawer were scattered. The newspaper lying on the bed had caused the whole mess.

Cindy struggled to reach the picture of her and Pete that had been on the nightstand and breathed a sigh of relief. The photograph and glass were both intact. She scanned the room to find her wheelchair beyond her reach against the closet door, where it had stopped after she had given it a shove in a rage after reading the headline on the comment section. *Unstable Marine Attacks Candidate Roberts*.

Her first reaction had been to fly into a rage. She flung the wheelchair aside and grabbed the walker without having full balance. That's when things went haywire.

"Oh, God, why is this happening to me?" Several tears mapped their way down her swollen cheek. She studied the 9mm automatic lying on the floor next to the nightstand and picked it up. The gun was fully loaded and ready to use.

Unstable? I can show you unstable.

By doing what? Another voice said inside her head. She laid the gun back on the floor as she heard the sound of Edith's SUV roll to a stop in the driveway. Cindy listened quietly as Edith opened and closed the passenger door. The rustle of grocery bags floated her way with the slamming of the screen door. A couple of minutes later came the knock on her bedroom door.

"Cindy? I'm back. Mind if I come in?"

Cindy laid the photograph aside and stared at the door.

"Cindy? Are you okay?"

Edith opened the door part way, then kicked the walker aside before entering the room. She gave the room a quick once-over before kneeling beside Cindy.

"What in the world...? Are you okay?"

Cynthia gave Edith a weak smile. "Couldn't get much worse, could it?"

"Things can always get worse if you let them," Edith said.

Edith got to her feet and set the nightstand upright, then began collecting its contents.

"Sorry I broke the lamp," Cindy said.

"Not a problem. I've got several more stored in the barn."

"I heard grocery bags. You went shopping after seeing Doctor Hastings."

"I did," Edith said with a nod. "I bought steaks and potatoes. I thought we could have the men barbeque tonight, so we won't have to cook."

"What did Doctor Hastings say about your tests?"

"He said my mammogram was good, and asked about you. Want me to tell him you're trying to walk on your own? That's what happened, wasn't it?"

Cindy handed Edith the picture.

"You can if you want. It's your house."

"It's yours too." Edith touched Cindy's cheek lightly and shook her head. "You're gonna have a nice shiner for a while. I just hope you didn't break something. You've been locked in here the past couple of days. Care to talk about it?"

Edith sat on the edge of the bed and gently rubbed the back of Cindy's head.

"Have you read the things they're saying about me?"

The Valley of Decision

She grabbed the newspaper in her fist and shook it in the air, before wadding it and throwing it across the room.

"The columnist says it was my fault. He says I was too possessive and drove Curt into Liz's arms. He says Curt was lucky to dump me, 'cause I'm crazy. I'm nothing but a joke. I called Pete yesterday, but they said he was in surgery. I left a message, but he hasn't called back, and I don't blame him. A crippled marine is useless. I don't know what I'm supposed to do with the rest of my life. Sit in that chair and rot, I guess. I was hoping that when I got out of the service, I'd become a cop, like Bobby, but that isn't gonna happen. I wish that sniper was a better shot and had killed me."

"Well," Edith exhaled slowly, "not everyone feels that way, honey. Doctor Hastings says he knows the man who wrote that column and says he is a friend of Curt's. I must have gotten a hundred calls from people wanting you to speak to their groups, and that bunch of teenage girls from the park are begging to come see you. They've started a Lieutenant Quentero fan club. I finally unplugged the phone. Peter may be a good doctor, but he's not too smart around women."

Edith knelt and folded Cindy in her arms, kissing the top of her head. Cindy kissed her on the cheek before handing her the 9mm pistol.

"You'd better hide this where I can't reach it."

Edith's eyes watered as she took to pistol.

"I had some unsettling thoughts while you were gone."

Edith kissed her on the cheek. "How can I help?"

"I don't know. Maybe the newspaper's right. I think I'm losing my mind sometimes. Help me, Mama. Please help me."

"I wish I could take it all away and make it better, but I can't. I'll tell you what," Edith held Cindy's cheeks between her palms, "the day after tomorrow's election day. And, there's a veteran's support meeting at the park. I think we should go. Let's go vote first and give Curt another black eye."

"No, I don't wanna see anyone. Oh, God, please help me. I'm going crazy."

"God's right here, baby, and He's not going anywhere." She kissed Cindy on the cheek, rocking her in her arms.

"And I'm right here beside you. You've faced tougher enemies than Curtis and survived. We'll get past this too. With God's help, we'll get through it."

Edith closed her eyes and started to pray while she held Cindy in her arms.

"God, help my baby girl. Give her strength and victory. Help her to put her complete trust in You and hold her head up high. In Jesus' name."

Chapter 45

Raymond Chandler leaned back in his plush office chair to study Curtis who was seated opposite him, with two black eyes and a bandage across his nose.

"I don't know what you expect me to do, Curt. You fired me. Now that you and Elizabeth have gone down in flames, you come running back to me. Why?"

"You're the guy with all the answers. I was hoping you could tell me what to do."

Raymond chuckled and shook his head. "I haven't the foggiest idea of what you should do. What do you want to do?"

"Carry on with the campaign. There's still some time. The election isn't until the day after tomorrow. I'll call a press conference this afternoon and explain what really happened."

Raymond laughed loudly this time. "I think they've got an idea what happened. Have you seen this?"

He clicked a remote and Zoe's video of him pulling at Cynthia and getting hit flooded the screen.

"Yeah, I've seen that," Curtis said sullenly.

"It went viral in forty-five minutes. You got a lot of publicity, Curt, just not the kind that gets people elected."

Raymond turned off the television and leaned forward.

"She's a Marine, Curt. You're lucky your nose is all she broke. So," he said with a sigh, "what are you going to do?"

"I was hoping you could help me."

Raymond got out of his chair and opened the door.

"Go home, Curt. Get on your knees and do some soul-searching. Forget about politics. Find out what it really means to turn your life over to Christ."

Chapter 46

Cindy parked her chair on the grass in the side yard so she could toss tennis balls for Jasper and Sally and still see Steven and Seth manning the grill. Miguel and Bobby had set a large folding table near the grill and was busy helping Edith stock it with plates and silverware. Karen had drug a lawn chair close to Cindy and turned Bobby Jr. loose to play with the dogs as she fed her daughter.

"It was nice of Edith to turn this into a family get-together," Karen said. "I just wish Peter could have made it."

"Becky said he might drop in later, if he can get someone to take his shift."

"That would be nice."

"Maybe," Cindy said with a grin. "He probably doesn't want to see me for a while."

"Oh, I'm sure he'd like to see you. He's been asking me how you're doing, anyway."

Cindy's stomach growled in spite of herself as the aroma of grilling steaks, garlic bread and ranch-style beans drifted her way. "Sorry 'bout that. I guess I'm hungry."

"That's okay. I'm starving myself," Karen said with a giggle.

Their attention was drawn toward the driveway as an old Toyota with faded red paint pulled through the gate and parked. Cindy quickly forgot the smell of the food as the doors opened and Fred Nunez and the girl with orange hair exited the car.

"What in the world?" Steven said. "Here," he shoved the long-handled barbeque fork toward Seth, "watch the meat while I see what's going on. And don't burn mine."

Fred raised both hands as Steven and Bobby Quentero marched toward them. "Sorry, we didn't know you were having a party. Zoe has something she wants to give Cynthia. We're not here to cause trouble; honest …"

Edith stepped in front of her husband. "Zoe? Is that your name?"

"Yes ma'am. Here…" She handed the picture wrapped in brown paper to Edith. "I think she'll like it. All of you will."

"Well, if that's the case, maybe *you* should give it to her."

"Here," Zoe took the picture from Edith and passed it to Cindy. "I took it the other night, and loved it so much I knew you had to have it."

"Thank you." Cindy smiled as she took the picture from Zoe.

"Hey, we match." Zoe stared at Cindy's swollen and discolored cheek. "Did Curt do that to you? Cause if he did, I can call some friends and…"

"No, no, I got this trying to walk by myself. I simply lost my balance and fell. The offer's kind of tempting, but I did it. Now, what do we have here?"

Cindy un-wrapped the picture and stared at her image in front of the American flag. "Wow!" she said after a moment. The photograph had captured the upper half of her uniform and medals, but it was the thoughtful expression on Cindy's face that drew her attention.

"Thank you. I do love it. Thank you so much."

"You took that?" Steven said as he leaned over Edith's shoulder.

"Yes, sir," Zoe said with a nod.

"You ought to have a studio somewhere and charge folks for your services."

"We plan to do that," she said, taking Fred's hand. "We've already got the place picked out."

"It's only a matter of a thing called money," Fred

said with a crooked grin.

"Yeah, it's always the same, ain't it?" Steven said as he turned away. "I'd better get back to the grill before the boys cremate the meat. You're welcome to stay."

"No, we didn't come here to crash your party," Fred said. "I tried calling, but you're phone's out of order."

"Yes, I don't know how it does it, but the receiver keeps unplugging it's self, and no one can call us."

"I really wouldn't know why either." Cindy looked away with a shrug.

"But both of you are more than welcome to stay," Edith said. "I always have more than enough to feed everyone, and I've got a couple of steaks in the refrigerator that will only take minutes to grill." She walked away yelling toward the boys. "Seth, Miguel...pull a couple more folding chairs out of the barn. We've got guests."

"She doesn't take no for an answer, does she?" Fred chuckled.

"She didn't even hear you," Cindy said, staring at the picture once more.

Zoe slowly wandered toward the grill as Fred and Cindy struck up a conversation like old friends. She stood to one side watching Steven and Seth as they seared the steaks. She couldn't remember ever eating steak, not even a single bite. The only steak she had eaten came ground up, but she had to admit the aroma made her hungry.

"Excuse me," she said as Seth returned from the kitchen with the extra steaks. "You don't need to cook me one. I'm vegan."

Steven stared at her for a couple of seconds. "Of course you are." He turned his attention back to the grill. "I'm not sure, but I think there's a cure for that sort of thing. I'll ask Pete when he gets here. He's a pretty good doctor."

"What?" Zoe scrunched her brow.

"Just kidding," Steven said with a laugh. "How long have you been a vegan?"

"I don't know. I've always been one. My mom's a

vegan."

"Oh, I understand," he said with a nod. "You came from a household of vegans."

"Yes, so we don't eat meat."

"Well, I reckon that might be okay, if you're bent that way. But I think I'll go ahead and grill this last steak in case Pete shows up. He loves a good steak, medium-rare."

Zoe turned to clear a space on the table for Edith to set a large bowl of potato salad.

"Seth?" Steven said as Zoe followed Mrs. Fowler back to the kitchen.

"Yes?"

"Do me a favor and grab a pack of Polish sausages from the refrigerator. I think we might need 'em. That girl's so skinny she's fixing to blow away in the wind. We need to pack a little weight on her bones."

******

"No, no, you just sit there and visit," Edith said at Fred's offer to help clean the table. The western sky had taken on a pink hue that would soon turn to crimson. Even though the afternoon temperature had been in the high seventies, the breeze had taken on a cool bite.

"There's something I need to ask you," Zoe said, placing her chair to face Cindy.

"Yes?" Cindy shifted in her chair to study Zoe's face.

"Fred says you used to teach a Bible class and you know about Jesus dying on the cross and all that stuff."

Cindy sat stunned for a few seconds. There wasn't an ounce of mockery in the statement, and she felt the girl was issuing a cry for help the best she knew how.

Cindy looked up at Fred and slowly shook her head. "That was a long time ago, Fred, and if I remember right, you used to laugh and poke fun at us."

"Yeah," he nodded. "I may have been laughing like everyone else, but some of us were really listening. I listened. My grandmother used to teach me about the Bible, so I understood a little more than the other guys."

She turned back to Zoe as a feeling of despair grew inside her own chest. The girl in front of her with orange hair, tattoos and piercings was in deep pain, and for the first time in years, Cindy began to see things clearly. "Come here," she held out her arms.

"Me?"

"Yes, come here." Cindy held the girl close as she prayed.

Oh God. Thank you so much for your love. Thank you for Jesus, being willing to die for our sins. Speak to Zoe, down deep in her heart. She's hurting, God. I can feel it. Heal her and fill her with love and peace. And give me the right words and wisdom to know the difference between what you want me to say and my own words. Amen."

She released her hold on Zoe and looked her in the eyes. "What is it that you want to know?"

"About what you just did. You talked to God just like you know Him. How do you do that? Are you some sort of saint or angel? That's what my mom says. That you have to be perfect for God to hear you, don't you?"

Cindy shook her head and chuckled. "I certainly hope not. I'm far from being a saint. Would you like to hear what the Bible says about that?"

"Yes, I would," Zoe said as Jennifer crawled into her lap.

"Jennifer," Karen reached for her daughter, but Zoe shook her head.

"No, it's okay. I like her being there."

"Well," Cindy said quietly. "In the Bible, the book of Romans chapter three, verse twenty three says everyone's a sinner. You, me, Fred, Karen—all of us have done something wrong in our lives, and that's what sin really is— doing something wrong. Romans six twenty-three says that what we earn or get for our sins is death— eternal separation from God."

"Fred says it's like God's on one side of the wall and we're on the other." Zoe said.

"Exactly. But in that same verse, it says God's gift to us is eternal life in Jesus. The cool part is, it's a gift. It's not something you can earn by being good.

"John chapter one, verse twelve says as many people who receive him, he gives them the right to become the children of God. Just as many as who believes in Him."

"All I've got to do is believe? What about all the bad stuff I've done?"

"First John, chapter one, verse nine says, if we confess our sins to God and tell Him all about the stuff we've done, he's faithful and righteous to forgive our sins and make us clean. Just like we've never done anything wrong."

"How?" A tear spilled over onto her cheek. "How do I do that?"

"Revelation chapter three, verse twenty says Jesus is standing at the door to your heart, wanting to come in, Zoe. He wants to give you a new life and take away all the bad stuff."

Zoe stared at Jennifer, who had gone to sleep in her lap. "I had a baby once."

From the expression on Fred's face, Cindy knew this was a revelation to him also.

"You did? What happened?"

"My mom and her boyfriend found out I was pregnant and gave me a good cussing, then made me have an abortion." She burst into tears. "Four years ago. I think about him every day, and I wonder what my baby's doing and if he's happy."

"Oh Zoe," Cindy took one of her hands, "I'm so sorry. Look at me, Zoe. The abortion may have been wrong, but God loves your baby."

"Really?"

"Yes, really. Your baby's in heaven right now with Jesus, and he's very, very, very happy, and he loves you so much. Would you like to pray and ask Jesus to come into your heart? I'll help you."

Zoe nodded as she accepted the box of tissues Edith offered.

"Fred? Come and help us.

Fred stared at her for a minute before kneeling beside Zoe while Cindy led them in prayer.

******

Cindy accepted the sweater but rejected the cup of coffee Edith offered. Becky and Bobby had taken their sleepy children home. Fred and Zoe had stayed a little longer as Zoe pelted Cindy with question after question before leaving. She had a feeling she would be seeing a lot of Zoe, but decided that was okay.

"Would you care for some company?" Edith asked.

"No, Mom. Thank you. I need to be alone right now. Is that okay?"

"Yes, that's perfectly fine." Edith leaned to kiss her cheek. "Don't stay up too late. We've got a big day tomorrow."

"Okay, thank you, Mom."

She waited until she was alone before looking heavenward. There was a full moon tonight amidst a blanket of stars. A few crickets chirped and a dog barked somewhere in the distance. She felt so full she thought she could burst.

She could clearly remember when she was younger and sitting in Mrs. Hanson's Sunday school class. Mrs. Hanson had been a missionary, and on special Sundays she would focus the lesson on foreign missions. A few times she brought missionaries into the class and discussed what it meant to be a missionary in a foreign land. Cindy could name the times she had raised her hand, promising to take the message of Jesus Christ to India or the far reaches of Africa. As an adult, she had gone on a different kind of mission overseas, but it was to deliver bullets and bombs, not the gospel. She still felt that mission was needed and just, but she had somehow gotten lost in the mix.

She shook her head and chuckled. Who had ever heard of a mission field right here, in the town you had grown up in? But the pain and guilt Zoe carried was very palpable, and she was only one of thousands within Cindy's reach.

Cindy felt the dam she had built inside burst as the tears came freely. She had never understood a lot about the prophet Joel, but this must be close to what he was talking about in chapter 3 verse 14 of his book, about the *"valley of decision."* God had brought her full-circle; now it was up to her to decide. Was she going to do what God wanted or pull away?

"Oh God, I am so…so sorry. You brought me home and laid an entire mission field at my feet, and I've ignored it. I've been too busy thinking of Curtis' campaign and of myself. And look at what it's brought me. I'm selfish and self-centered, and I've really made a mess of things, haven't I? Even Pete won't talk to me anymore. Forgive me, Lord. Please forgive me."

Chapter 47

"Hey, you two," Steven hollered at the boys mucking stalls. "Pile in the truck."

"Where are we going?" Seth yelled back.

"We're gonna go vote. Those stalls can wait 'til we get back."

"I don't know," Miguel said, shaking his head. "I don't think we smell too good."

"So? You just smell like politics. Pile in. I'll tell Edith we're leaving."

"Hold your horses," Edith yelled from the porch. "Let me collect Cindy and put her chair in the car and we'll follow you."

Steven waited until Cindy was buckled in, and then placed her chair in the back of the Expedition.

"All set," he said, slamming the rear hatch.

"We'll be right behind you. Then, we're going to take part in the veteran's gathering in the park at noon."

******

Cindy hated to admit it, but it gave her a small surge of pleasure voting for Curtis' opponent. She said a quick prayer, asking God to help her not to gloat.

Edith drove to the park and stopped at the curb, then stood with her hands on her hips as Steven parked behind her.

"I thought you had to go back home. What are you doing here?"

"I got to thinking. Me and the boys have to eat anyway, and I'm a veteran. Why not eat first, then go home?"

"You could've told me up front and we could have all ridden together."

Seth helped Cindy into her chair, and then turned to help his mother carry things to the tables. Cindy rolled part way then stopped to survey the small gathering around a couple of picnic tables. Several children were playing a game of tag. A large banner was hanging between two trees that read WELCOME VETERANS. Cindy rolled her chair toward a group of men and women who were either in wheelchairs or using crutches. One beautiful woman had lost both of her legs. A big man was cooking hamburgers and hot dogs on a grill while three women set bowls of potato salad and chips on the tables. It took all of sixty seconds for Edith to set a large bowl of ranch beans on the table and introduce herself to the women.

"Thank you. We need all the help we can get," one of the women said.

"You've got it," Edith said. "Where do you want me?"

Cindy was taken aback as the veterans cheered her arrival and welcomed her into their group.

"Yeah, I think everyone of us saw the video of you belting Curt," said a Marine holding a can of beer.

"I was a little disappointed," the woman with missing legs said.

"Disappointed?" one of the men asked.

"Yeah, I was hoping she'd belt him again."

"Well, I did…sort of." Cindy said. "I voted for the other guy this morning." That brought another round of cheers.

Steven sent Seth and Miguel to the store for more hotdogs and buns then joined the man at the grill.

"I'm Steve," he said, offering his hand. "Would you mind some help?"

"Glad for the hand. You can do the dogs while I flip burgers. My name's Ben." He eyed Steven a short minute. "Vietnam?"

"Yes sir," Steven said with a nod. "You too?"

"Yeah. It's good they've got things like this now to help these kids. We had some help through the V.A., but I don't remember anything like this."

"No. We made it by the grace of God and hard work."

"That was a different time and a different war. A lot of people, especially the dope-smoking college set, didn't want us there. I got called all kinds of names when I got home."

"Yeah, me too," Steven said with a snort. "I got mustered out in San Francisco, and wanted to see a little bit of the city before I left. As I was leaving the Presidio in my uniform, some young guy decided to call me a baby-killer and spit in my face."

"And what'd you do?"

"He was shy a couple of teeth, and I got to spend the night in the brig. Looking back at it, I reckon I was lucky there were a couple of MPs nearby. There were a dozen or so radical hippies there who saw me hit him, and decided to take a dislike toward me."

They turned as the small crowd of veterans roared with laughter.

"Well, she certainly fit right in," Ben said. "Most of the time, it takes a few weeks before they start trusting anyone.

"Well, Cindy's like that. I don't think she trusts folks any easier than the rest, especially after Curtis Roberts. But she does know how to talk to people."

The lady in charge had lost her son in Iraq, and kept the meeting informal and light, hoping the vets would meet and make new friends and build a support group. Cindy received the opportunity to share her experience and closed the meeting with prayer.

******

Steven scooted his chair closer to the kitchen table and opened the morning paper.

"Huh! I guess that's no surprise."

"What's that?" Edith asked as she came to the table with a fresh pot of coffee.

"This." He unfolded the front page on the table.

Edith stopped to study the headlines before suppressing a giggle. "I must say I'm not surprised."

Cindy leaned to see what everyone was talking about. The headlines were in bold type across the front page.

ROBERTS LOSES IN LANDSLIDE

"I guess I should feel sorry for him, but I don't." Cindy shrugged as she buttered her toast.

She pulled back as Edith and Steven both stared at her.

"What? I called and left a message saying I was sorry for breaking his nose. I didn't mean to hurt him. I just wanted him out of my face."

They were still staring.

"Okay, would praying for him be good enough for now?"

"Praying for him would be fine," Edith said with a smile.

******

The young therapist named Gloria placed a rubber ball halfway to the opposite wall inside the therapy room and smiled.

"We've got the room to ourselves today, so I want you to try some things we haven't done before. I know you haven't gone this far in our walks, but I want you walk to the ball and kick it. Think you can do it?"

Cindy gave her a crooked smile as Edith gripped the

belt and helped her stand. "We'll find out, won't we?"

"Come on now. Take your time," Gloria said. "That's good. Keep coming."

Beads of sweat popped out on Cynthia's brow as she gripped the walker and swung both legs forward, using her arms to support her weight. The room seemed to grow longer as she struggled forward. Gloria stayed a matter of inches in front of her, urging her onward. Cindy gritted her teeth as a vision of her old drill sergeant appeared in front of her, yelling and shouting obscenities, telling the squad what a worthless bunch of garbage they were. Cindy swung her legs farther with each effort until finally, Gloria was telling her to stop.

"Very good, Cindy." She stepped to one side. "Now, I want you to kick the ball with one foot."

"I can't. I can't move my legs. I tried and they don't work."

"Sure you can. You just *think* you can't."

"I'm telling you I can't," Cindy snapped.

"You can try," Gloria said as she stood behind the ball. "Come on, kick it." Gloria heaved a sigh. "I didn't think Marines quit so easily."

Cindy clenched her jaw and swung forward, kicking the ball with both feet.

"That's good," Gloria said as she picked up the ball. She quickly replaced it in front of Cindy and stepped back. "One foot now. Hurry." Cindy again kicked it with both feet. Gloria repeatedly replaced the ball several more times, urging her to kick with one leg.

Cindy kept moving forward and kicking as the vision of her drill sergeant reappeared where Gloria was supposed to be. Then, Edith and Gloria both squealed in excitement.

"See? I told you, you could do it. You kicked the ball with you right foot." Gloria bounced up and down. She placed the ball behind Edith and grinned.

"Now, let's do it back to the beginning."

Chapter 48

"What in the world?" Edith stared out the screen door as a beat-up Chevy rattled past the house leaving a trail of blue smoke before turning though the gate. Jasper, who was taking a nap on the front porch, jerked his head upward and dashed toward the barn. The engine was making a loud knocking noise as the car rolled to a stop in the driveway, where it gave a final shudder and gave up the ghost. The Chevy had once been white, but now was sporting a black front fender and hood with large patches of rust.

"What was that?" Steven had just come from the back of the house to refill his coffee mug.

"Take a look."

He stared over Edith's head as the car doors opened and Zoe, along with four other kids, climbed out. All of them were sporting tattoos and piercings.

"Wonder what they want?

"Cindy said something about having a Bible study with Zoe this afternoon," Edith said.

"Well, I reckon you'd better warn her while I greet our guests."

The car was now hissing as a combination of smoke and steam rolled from beneath the hood.

"I hope that thing doesn't suffocate the horses," Steven said with a snort.

"Just be patient." Edith laid a hand on Steven's shoulder. "Remember we're representing Christ."

"I ain't got a problem with Cindy teaching kids about Jesus here at the ranch. I just want them to move that old car

The Valley of Decision

before it explodes and kills the horses."

Steven took a sip of coffee as Edith disappeared down the hall. He grinned as Zoe waved, and placed his coffee mug on the porch railing before descending the steps toward the car.

"Hi Mr. Fowler. I brought some friends to hear about God. I hope that's okay." The smile on the girl's face caught him off guard. It wasn't the same sullen girl that had given Cindy the photograph a couple of days ago.

"It's nice to see you again. I need you folks to do something real quick. I need you to move this car back about ten or twelve feet over yonder," he said, pointing toward a wide graveled area.

"Are you expecting more company? We can come back later," Zoe said wistfully.

"No, you folks are just fine. It's just that this thing is still hissing and smoking, and you're parked right next to a pen of horses. It could hurt the horses if they breathe some of that smoke, or if it goes up in flames. So, could you just see if it will start and back it up some?"

"Sure, no problem."

Zoe pulled the key from her jeans pocket and inserted it into the ignition, but only received a click. She tried several more times before Steven told her it was okay.

Steven grabbed a couple of saddles blankets that were hanging on the corral drying. "Zoe? Make sure the car's in neutral. And you boys, spread these blankets on the hood so you don't burn your hands."

He waited while they covered the hood.

"Now, push!" The boys grunted as they pushed and strained, moving the car several inches, only to have it roll back when they stopped to catch their breaths.

"Alright, lean into it this time." Steven found a spot between two boys and leaned into the car himself. The car seemed to roll easily toward the graveled parking space.

"That's good. Right here."

"That was easy once he started pushing," one of the

boys said with a laugh.

"It's always easier when folks help each other," Steven said. "Now, I see Cindy's on the porch, so let's go see her."

He draped his hand on one of Zoe's shoulders as they headed toward the house. He waited while she introduced everyone.

"Okay," Steven said, "where are you holding this study?"

"It's a nice day. How about right here on the porch?" Cindy said.

"Sounds good to me. Come on, you two," he motioned toward the two boys, "follow me." He led the boys to the barn for folding chairs. Once they had the chairs set, he joined Edith inside the kitchen.

"We'd better be prepared for this to be a weekly event. They seem to be getting along well," Edith said as the group on the front porch laughed.

"Think I ought to fire up the grill? It's already twelve-thirty."

"Mmm, probably so. I think we've still got a couple of packages of hot links and buns in the freezer. I'll defrost them in the microwave. You might check the cupboard also. I think there's a family-sized can of chili somewhere."

"Yeah, and I'm pretty sure we've got a bag of corn chips around here somewhere," Steve said as he poked his head into the freezer.

******

"The west wasn't won on rabbit food." Steven had been trying to get Zoe to at least taste one of the hot links then maybe, if she at least tasted the flavor, she might be willing to add a little meat to her diet. Zoe only shook her head no,

"Well, how do you know if you don't like it, if you've never tried something?"

"I've never eaten mud, but I know I wouldn't like it," Zoe said.

"Being a vegan is like a religion with Zoe," a boy named Bill said before chomping a hot link.

"That right?" Steven asked her.

"It isn't like that…really," she said with a scowl.

"Oh? Well, what is it then?"

"I've tasted meat on occasion. I ate a piece of bacon just the other day. I just don't do it very often."

"Hmmm," Steven said, cocking his head to one side. "Then, what would it take to get you to bite this hot link?" He waved the bun under her nose.

"Here, give me that." Zoe grabbed a hot link from Steven's grasp and added mustard, chopped onion, relish and some shredded cheese like she'd been doing it all her life. She glared at Steven as she took a bite and chewed. "Satisfied?"

"Well, I see it didn't kill you," Steven said with a snort. "What do you have against eating meat?"

"You have to kill an animal to make one of these," she held the link in front of Steven's face, "and I don't want to think about that."

"Oh," Steven said with a nod. "I can understand that. You do realize, don't you, that Jesus ate meat while he was here on this earth?"

"No," she shook her head.

"Oh, yes he did. Ask Cindy, if you don't believe me."

"Cindy?" Zoe turned toward Cindy who grinned and slowly nodded.

Steven took the last links from the grill and gave Zoe a crooked grin. "I wouldn't steer you wrong or hurt you for the world. I just want you to understand that some things we've been taught or believe might not be exactly the way things really are. Like eating or not eating that link. I don't think Jesus was committing a sin when he ate a slice of beef. Do you?"

Zoe gave Steven a scowl before taking another bite.

"Satisfied?" she said as she chewed vigorously.

"If you feel like you need to spit it out, that's okay, honey," Edith said. "Sometimes my husband gets a little abrupt and says things he shouldn't.

Zoe chewed a little more and swallowed as one of the boys started a little chant.

Go Zoe go! Go Zoe go!"

Pretty soon, all the kids were stomping their feet as they chanted.

"Go Zoe go! Go Zoe go."

Zoe held the bun and link up and grinned as she took another bite. She quickly devoured the rest of the link and wiped her mouth on a paper napkin. "Sometimes," she said to Steven, "you don't have much choice of what you eat. Especially when you're on the streets. You simply eat what you can find."

"Yeah," a girl named Dawn said. "If you can time it just right, you can find some pretty good stuff in the dumpster behind *Liu's Market*."

"Yeah, he tosses some pretty good fruit and veggies to make room for fresh stuff," another girl said. "That's when Zoe can eat like a true vegan."

"Excuse me, I'll be right back," Steven said and walked briskly toward the kitchen as the kids kept talking about dumpster diving.

Edith waited a moment before following, and found him standing by the sink, wiping his eyes on a paper towel.

"Steven? What's wrong?"

He looked at her through watery eyes. "Didn't you hear them talk about living on garbage?"

"Yes, I did," Edith said with a nod.

"Well, it just got to me, that's all."

"I know," she said, hugging him around the waist. "All we can do is our part, and make sure they get a home-cooked meal once in a while. Now, come on," she patted him on the chest, "let's go show them we really do love them."

"Be right behind you," Steven said as he blew his

nose.

"Is Dad okay?" Cindy asked as Edith rejoined the group.

"Oh, he's just fine. He got something in his eye. See?" she said as Steven allowed the screen door to bang shut behind him. "Here he comes now."

Seth and Miguel pulled into the yard and parked the four-wheeler beside the John Deere tractor near the barn. They joined the group on the front porch, eying the food on the folding table.

"I know you boys are hungry, so you'd better dig in before Zoe and her friends polish it off," Edith said.

"How's the fence coming along?" Steven asked as he set two cans of cold soda on the table.

"Fence is done," Seth said as he grabbed two hot links and buns. "I guess whoever flattened it may have given himself a bigger problem than he left with us."

"How's that?"

"Miguel found engine oil on one of the broken posts."

"In that case, we'd best check the ground for oil. We don't want any of the cattle getting sick."

"I already did that," Miguel said, "and tossed it into the quad."

"Good man…both of you. Now, eat your lunch."

Chapter 49

Zoe sat dejectedly in the front passenger seat of Edith's Expedition. Her car simply would not start, no matter how she prayed, begged and even threatened. Seth finally took a look at the engine and crawled under the car. He looked at her sadly and slowly shook his head as he wiped his hands.

"Sorry Zoe, but it's not going to start. You threw a rod through the engine block."

"What's that mean?" she asked.

"What it means is," he took her hand and pulled her down to sit on her heels as he pointed. "You have a big hole in the side of the motor. See that dark spot on the gravel?"

"Yes."

"That your engine oil. If you look back near the corral, you can see a trail where you were leaking."

"So, what can I do to fix it?"

"What he's saying, Zoe, is it needs a new motor, and that would cost more than the car's worth," Steven said.

"I guess Fred's friend was right," she said dejectedly. "He said it wasn't going to run much longer, but I didn't think it was going to die this soon."

That was thirty minutes ago. Now, she sat staring out the window as Edith drove her and her friends home.

"I'm really sorry about this, Mrs. Fowler."

"That's alright, Zoe. I didn't have a whole lot to do this afternoon."

"I guess we won't be coming back for Bible study next week," Zoe said bitterly.

"And, why's that?" Edith glanced at her through the corner of her eye.

"I don't have a car, and it's too far to walk. I can't even go to work. That's why."

"Oh," Edith nodded. "Well, I hope you don't think we're going to let a little thing like a broken car stand in our way. God will work something out. You'll see."

"I won't be a burden to you and Mr. Fowler. I won't come if that's the case."

"Like I said," Edith heaved a sigh, "God will work something out."

She glanced at Zoe and smiled.

******

"Look at you! You're doing great," Gloria said as Cindy kicked the ball with her right foot. It wasn't a clean kick, and the ball kind of rolled to the right a few feet before stopping, but it was still a kick.

Edith had loaded Cindy into the Expedition as soon as she had gotten home, and they arrived ten minutes late for her appointment.

Gloria reset the ball and stared at Cindy. "What? No cheer? Not even a smile? You're doing really great. What's wrong? Aren't you feeling good?"

"Huh? Oh, I'm sorry. My mind was somewhere else."

"Well, let's see if we can kick the ball with your left foot this time. We've only got fifteen more minutes before I see another client."

"Okay." Cindy crow-hopped forward with the walker and gave the ball a sound kick with her left foot.

"See? That's what we're looking for. I want to see you do that with both feet. You need to practice this at home thirty minutes a day."

Gloria placed the ball on the floor and looked at Cindy carefully.

"What's on your mind? I hope Curtis Roberts isn't causing you more trouble."

"No, thank God it's not that," Cindy said with a laugh. She crow-hopped forward and kicked the ball with her right foot and heaved a sigh of disgust as the ball dribbled a few feet to the right.

"You definitely have more control with you left leg," Gloria said.

"I have a little feeling creeping back into it."

"Really?" Gloria grinned. "What's it feel like?"

"Like my whole leg is asleep. It drives me crazy when I'm trying to sleep. But I'll take it."

Gloria replaced the ball on the floor. "You were saying about your somber mood?"

"I started doing a Bible study at the ranch for a group of teens. We're just getting started, and one of the girls said she would provide the rides to the ranch in her old car."

Cindy crow-hopped forward and kicked at the ball with her left foot.

"That sounds good. What's the problem?" Gloria said and moved behind the ball.

"The problem is," Edith said, "her friend's car gave up the ghost this afternoon, and she can't afford to buy another one."

"Oh, that can be a problem. Well," Gloria said as she placed the ball back into a bin, "I hate to break this up, but my next client is here. Remember what I said and do this every day. Oh, and practice moving one leg at a time instead of hopping. Make a game out of it. You're doing very well."

Chapter 50

Cindy sat upright in bed staring at the pictures on the walls. There was one of her racing *Kiowa Dawn* around a barrel at the Oakdale rodeo. That was almost a perfect run and they had won the first place trophy that day. She loved that horse and rode him every chance she got. She hadn't been to the barn to see him in over two weeks now. She hadn't seen her truck since she'd been home. The wheels on her wheelchair sunk in the graveled driveway, making it almost impossible to cross without help.

There's no sense in looking at either one, since I can't ride a horse or drive.

She slammed her Bible shut and gritted her teeth.

I know I promised you I'd go on a mission field if you asked. But I thought I'd be able to walk, and even run, and drive myself where I needed to go. Now, I even need someone with me when I go to the bathroom. Do you have any idea how embarrassing that is?

Cindy wiped the corner of her eyes against her pajama sleeves. The first thing that popped into her head when Zoe's old car wouldn't start was her own Ford diesel-powered truck. She had worked like a slave in the hot sun, building fences and bucking hay, and saved every dime including what she won from the rodeo circuit in order to buy that truck. Then she made sure it got washed and waxed every week.

It isn't fair; you know that, don't you? You've taken everything I love from me, except the truck, and now you want that too?

The voice whispered inside her head once more, causing a flood of tears to come.

How much do you love me, Cynthia? I gave everything for you, including my life.

"Aggh!" Cindy growled through clenched teeth. "Dying would have been easy. I was willing to do that when I put on the uniform. Dying would have been a piece of cake. Why didn't you just let that happen?"

Because you're right. Dying would have been easy for you. But can you give up everything and live for me, Cynthia? Just how much do you really love me?

Chapter 51

Edith had to beg and plead when she had shown up at Fred's door the following day. It wasn't easy to get Zoe into the Expedition. Even now, the girl sat staring out the window sullenly as Edith guided the SUV down Briggsmore Ave.

"Do you know where the title and registration cards are for your car?"

"Registration is in the glovebox, and I've got the title in my wallet. Why?"

"Steven was thinking of calling a salvage yard for you."

"I can take care of that myself."

"Okay." Edith stopped at a red light and sat quietly. The light changed and she accelerated slowly and turned north toward the ranch.

"Who's going to be there?" Zoe said, breaking her self-imposed silence.

"Just family. You and me…Steve, Cindy, Seth and Miguel. Why?"

"I just don't want to see or talk to anyone. Besides, I'm not family."

"We tend to think of you as family. But I understand what you're saying." She gave Zoe a smile as her cell phone rang. She pulled onto the shoulder to answer.

"Hello? Yes, I'm almost there. Really? You're sure about this? That's quite a present. No, we're almost there. Bye."

"You really should take me home, Mrs. Fowler. I won't be much company, and I really need to be alone right now."

"Okay, but we're almost there, and you need to see Cindy for a few minutes. It has something to do with your car."

"Like what? They've found a place to bury it? I know it isn't much, but I bought it myself with my own money. It's hard to understand."

"No, I know exactly how you feel. I watched Cindy work as hard as any man, slaving away to buy her own vehicle. And I did pretty much the same thing with this old car. She may be getting old, but she's mine." She smiled at Zoe with an air of pride and nodded.

"I know exactly how you feel. I would too."

Chapter 52

Cindy gave herself a running start by racing her chair down the ramp as fast as she dared, only to have the wheels sink in the gravel. She struggled to work her chair across the graveled driveway toward the barn, and had worked up a good sweat by the time the roar of the quad caused her to turn her head. Seth and Miguel wheeled into the yard and parked beside the tack house.

"Need a hand?" Seth asked.

"That would be nice. These small front wheels don't navigate gravel too well."

"We can fix that." He grabbed the handles and tipped her chair back a few inches, then pulled her easily backwards into the barn. "Looking for something in particular?"

"Yes, I am. I need you two guys to uncover my truck and see if it will start."

"No problem," Miguel said with a grin. "Seth's dad's been starting it once a week while you were gone. We drove it around the ranch a couple of times when Seth's truck was in the garage getting fixed."

"Cool," she said with a nod, then stopped to glare. "I hope you didn't scratch it."

"Not a chance," Seth said with a loud laugh. "Like I'd scratch your truck, when you can pick me off at two-hundred yards with a .30-06.

"Pull it out of the barn for me, please."

"Why, you gonna try driving it?" Seth chuckled.

"I wish. No, I want to see if Zoe might want it."

"Zoe? Does she have that kind of money?"

"I really don't know." Cindy laughed. "I know it sounds crazy, but I keep getting a feeling that God wants her to have it. Pull it outside and we'll find out."

The boys removed the tarp covering the garnet-blue three-quarter ton Ford pickup and Miguel climbed into the driver's seat. The engine started with the first turn of the key and Miguel pulled the truck out of the barn and left it idling in the driveway.

"Thank you guys. Now, can one of you give me a hand with this stupid chair?"

"Sure." Seth tilted the chair and rolled her toward the house and parked her on the concrete. A few minutes later, Edith's Expedition rolled through the gate and parked near Cindy.

Zoe climbed out of the car and stared at the blue truck idling in the driveway before walking toward Cindy.

"Nice truck," Zoe said with a nod toward the truck. "Who's is it?"

"Mine," Cindy said. "It's been stuck inside the barn ever since I got sent to Afghanistan. I used it to pull the horse trailer while I was riding the rodeo circuit. I don't think I'll be driving any more, at least not for a long while."

"That's too bad. It's a pretty truck," Zoe said. "Mrs. Fowler said you wanted to talk to me? What about? Did I do something wrong?"

"No, no," Cindy shook her head. "I was wondering if you would like the truck?"

"What?!!" Seth said loudly. "You're really going to give it to her? I thought you were joking."

"I'd say that's a pretty good gift," Steven said as he joined them. "Are you sure? You could sell that truck for a pretty penny."

"Yes, but then I wouldn't be doing what God told me to do." Cindy gave him a crooked smile.

"You've got to be kidding," Zoe said. "Thanks, but I can't afford to buy your truck. I work behind the counter at the theater."

"Not for long. You and Fred are going to open your studio, remember? And I didn't ask if you wanted to *buy* it. I asked if you *wanted* it."

"You've got to be kidding. 'Cause if you're not, I...I...don't know what to say."

"Well, I'll tell you what," Steven said, patting Zoe on the back. "Let's take it for a spin and see how you really like it before you make any decisions. It has full power and air, with an automatic transmission. You're driving, so climb in."

Cindy felt a combination of joy and sadness sweep over her as the truck rolled onto the field road and away from the yard.

"Why don't you give me the truck, and I'll give her mine," Seth said.

"Several reasons," Cindy said with a laugh. "First of all, you have yours jacked up so high, I'd need a step ladder to get inside, even if I had two good legs. Second, I've seen you drive, and no telling what shape your truck is really in. Besides, I've prayed about it, and I believe this is what God wants me to do."

"Well, you boys come with me and let's see what we can do about dinner," Edith said. "I'm kind of hungry."

"Can you believe that," Seth's voice carried back to her as they went inside the house. "She's really going to give her the truck."

"It's her truck to give," Miguel said with a chuckle.

******

Zoe called Fred, who came at once and spent twenty minutes staring at the truck, then another fifteen minutes holding Zoe in his arms as she broke into sobs.

"I can't believe you're doing this," he said to Cindy. "She's a great girl, but she's still got some rough edges, even after asking Jesus into her heart."

"Don't we all, Fred?" Cindy said with a chuckle. "She's not a bigger sinner than I am. Sin is sin, no matter how you try to dress it up. Speaking of which, Dad's been wondering whatever happened to Elizabeth Sparks? She hasn't been on TV since the mess at The Gallo Center."

"She got canned," Fred said with a snicker.

"Really?"

"Yeah, but she's like an alley cat, and will eventually land on her feet somewhere. And no one's heard from or seen Curt at all. It's like he's disappeared."

"Maybe an alien spaceship beamed him up."

They both laughed and sat watching Zoe at the grill. Steven handed her the long-handled spatula while he went into the kitchen to refill his coffee mug. Fred chuckled as she flipped the hamburger patties like a pro.

"By the way," Cindy said as an afterthought. "Zoe's living in your house, isn't she?"

"Yeah, but it's not what you think. She's got her own bedroom, and I've got mine."

"Really? Now, that's a novel idea," she said thoughtfully. "Exactly what are your plans for her?"

"I don't know," he said, staring at Zoe as Steven rejoined her at the grill. Zoe kept the spatula as he sipped his coffee. "All I know is, I was somehow supposed to be connected with her the minute I saw her behind the counter when I ordered a slice of pizza and hot buttered popcorn." He looked at Cindy seriously. "She's brilliant. Her mind never stops working. That video going viral was Zoe's doing. She filmed it and posted it on the internet. When she did, she included a little blurb at the end, saying it was courtesy of *Fred and Zoe's Photography* and included my website and cellphone number. I've gotten calls from hundreds of people wanting to have pictures taken. I quit my job at the station today to take care of them. She asks so many Bible questions that I don't know the answers to, I've started reading my grandmother's Bible again and praying. But I'll admit it. I'm doing a lousy job of it." He heaved a sigh and smiled.

"Like I said, I knew the instant I saw her, I was

supposed to be with her. It's hard to explain. Kinda like a knowing, deep inside."

"I know the feeling well, Fred," Cindy said with a slow nod. "It's the same feeling I have about the truck. I'd say you just got a message from God. Take special care of her, Fred. She's a gift from God."

Fred stared at Cindy for a long minute as his eyes misted over.

"Wow! I never thought of it that way. I guess I'd better marry her." He sniffed and wiped the corners of his eyes with his fingers. "Want to help plan a wedding?"

******

Cindy sat upright in bed reading her Bible. She just happened to be studying the eleventh chapter of Hebrews. Most people refer to that chapter as the *Faith Chapter*, or the *Gallery of Faith*. Whatever people chose to call it, Cindy had always loved those verses. But, tonight she was struck with the fact that all the people mentioned in the chapter had given everything they owned or loved in order to follow God. She closed the Bible as tears welled in her eyes and heaved a deep moan.

"Oh, God, I am so, so sorry for being hard-hearted, and hard-headed. I promised you years ago I'd go and do what you asked in order to tell others about you. Instead, I joined the Marines. It took you awhile to bring me back, but that's not your fault. It's mine. Giving Zoe that truck was one of the hardest things I've done. You know how I loved that truck. But, I'm asking you to bless it, and keep it running good, and bless Zoe's efforts to bring hurting kids into your kingdom. Please tell me if there is anything else standing in my way. Amen."

******

If there was any trepidation in her heart about Zoe

not taking care of the truck, or not using it for God's glory, those fears vanished the next Tuesday when she parked the truck and six kids piled out. A beat-up Toyota parked next to her and four more piled out. A grin crept across Cindy's lips as Zoe headed toward the house. She had cropped all of her hair short and was sporting jeans, cowgirl boots, hat and an engagement ring.

Edith had called Pastor Gifford, telling him about Cindy's Bible studies and invited him to sit in to see what was transpiring and see if he had any suggestions. He stood beside Edith on the front porch as Steven guided the group toward the barn.

"Hey, y'all, there's too many of you to sit on the front porch. Come on into the barn. We've already got chairs, coffee and hot chocolate waiting. But there's no smoking allowed, 'cause we don't want the barn to burn down."

Steven paused and gave Zoe the once-over, from hat to boots. "Well now, look at you. What caused the big change?"

"Well, I saw that picture of Cindy standing by the truck in the hallway, and realized it was a cowgirl's truck. I thought I'd dress appropriately. Why? Don't you like it?"

"No, quite the contrary. I think you make a real pretty cowgirl."

"Thanks." She hugged Steven around the waist as a smile lit her face. "I never met my dad or grandpa. Would you mind if I called you Grandpa?"

Steven hugged her tighter. "No, Zoe. I'd be honored to have you as my granddaughter.

Pastor Gifford cleared his throat and took Edith aside. "And you feed them lunch when they're finished?"

"That's been the plan," Edith said, then laughed. "Actually, there isn't a plan. We just kind of did what we thought needed doing. It wasn't too bad at first with a small group, but it's been getting bigger. You can expect more next Tuesday."

"I don't want you doing all this by yourselves. You'll burn out. These kids need the gospel, and I doubt they'll get it inside a church. They're not going to attend a traditional church. They'll get the gospel exactly like you're doing. I'll get a few of the ladies at the church to help with the feeding and cleaning. Do you think Cindy will care if I sit in and listen?"

"I don't see why. Go right ahead."

He paused and grinned. "Ah, what's the name of the cowgirl who drove the blue truck?"

"That's Zoe Shultz. She has quite a story of her own. I'll tell you about her sometime. She's engaged to a fine young man, and I'm pretty sure they'll want to get married here on the ranch. Feel like doing a wedding with cattle mooing and horses neighing in the background?"

"I'm sure that can be arranged," he said with a chuckle. The group inside the barn laughed at something Cindy said.

"Well, I guess I'd better see if I can slip in without disturbing their Bible study."

******

The sound of a heavy truck pulling into the yard followed by a tractor being unloaded caused Cindy to abandon her bookkeeping chore and wheel her chair to the front door and pull it open.

"Mom?" she said loudly as a beat-up pickup with a crew cab parked near the gate and four men piled out.

"Mom?" she repeated louder.

"Yes?" Edit said, coming from the kitchen.

"What's going on out there?

"Why don't we go out and see?"

Edith held the screen door open for Cindy as she wheeled onto the front porch. They saw Steven pull into the yard and park on the grassy area on the opposite side of the house. He was talking to one of the men and making hand motions.

"What are they doing?"

"Well...," Edith drug the word out. "He's finally decided to pour a concrete pad between the house and barn. Something that should've been done years ago."

"What made him decide to do that now? I must've asked him to do that a hundred times myself, before I joined the Marines. I had to wade through a lake of mud every winter taking care of the horses."

"And I got tired of the boys tromping through the house in muddy boots," Edith said.

The man Steven talked to made some lines with white paint from the barn to the house and the tractor immediately began scooping dirt and gravel and piling it at the side of the barn.

"I'm glad he's doing it, but why now?"

"Because Seth told him you couldn't go to the barn and see Kiowa Dawn. He got to thinking about it and started feeling really bad."

"Huh," Cindy looked back toward the tractor as it dug another scoop. "I wonder how my walker will do on it?"

"We can find out in a couple of days." Edith gave her a warm smile.

"I'll have the boys store some hay and grain low and you can start feeding Kiowa yourself. How's that sound?"

"Fine. Yeah, I think I'd like that."

Chapter 53

Curtis sat slumped over the bar, nursing a whisky sour. He had discovered the tiny bar tucked between a motorcycle repair shop and an adult bookstore when he had gotten turned around one evening while driving to his campaign headquarters. He had been licking his wounds after giving a less than stellar speech to a roomful of warehouse workers. He parked and stepped inside for a quick one, and found a quiet establishment where no one bothered anyone with stupid questions. Stopping for a drink at Mindy's had quickly become a habit. That was before he met Cindy Quentero and her brother in front of the hospital. Then things began changing at lightning speed.

It was actually Elizabeth Sparks who made the changes. She recognized Cindy's value to his campaign and used her like a director would use a well-seasoned actress, without Cindy knowing she was being used.

Curtis was skeptical at first.

"You want me to do what?" He laughed loudly, causing several diners inside The Bamboo Palace to turn and stare.

"You've dated her before, so it shouldn't be too hard to do it again. Look," she added as Curtis shook his head and snickered, "all I'm asking is to play along until after the election. Then," she shrugged. "You can break it off. It happens all the time. Right?"

It was actually working, and his ratings seemed to climb a little higher with every polling, even while refusing to participate in the debates. He passed Walters in the polls two days before the Gallo Center fiasco.

"Charlie Hough," Curtis mumbled out loud. "It was Charlie's fault."

"What was that?" Mindy paused wiping the bar with a damp towel to look his way.

"Nothing. Just talking to myself." He tossed off the last of his whisky sour and slid the glass to the middle of the bar. "I'll take another one of those."

Mindy stared at Curtis carefully as she picked up the glass. "No," she shook her head slowly, "I think you're way past your limit."

"Don't tell me when I've had enough. I'm tired of women telling me what to do. Give me another whisky."

"No, you just proved my point. Your speech is slurred and now you're wanting to argue for the first time since you've been coming in here. I could lose my license selling you another drink. Let me call you a cab, so you can go home and sleep it off."

"I don't need a cab. I know the way to my house."

Curtis almost fell sliding off the barstool.

"I'm calling a cab. Go sit in a booth." Mindy picked up the phone and began punching numbers. Curtis ignored her and straightened his jacket as he staggered out the door. Mindy shook her head and ended the call for a cab and called the police instead.

Curtis mumbled a couple of curses as he fumbled with the remote, trying to open the driver's door. "There we are," he said as he found the right button. Once ensconced behind the wheel, he inserted the key and the powerful Cadillac engine roared to life. He backed out of the parking stall, almost hitting a Dodge pickup, and pulled slowly forward.

Drive slowly, he told himself. *Just like college. Drive slow and careful and no one will ever know you've had a drink or two.* He uttered another curse as he drove off the curb leaving the parking lot. He had only gone a half a block toward McHenry Ave when he noticed the red and blue flashing lights behind him.

******

Officers Cruz and McFarland had stopped at Denny's for two coffees to go when the call came in. *Unruly intoxicated driver leaving Mindy's Bar.* Mindy's sat approximately two blocks from Denny's, so they took the call. They had just turned past the motorcycle repair shop when Curt pulled out of the lot.

"Yeah, he's smashed." Cruz flipped on the lights as Curtis drove over the curb. Instead of pulling over the Cadillac sped toward McHenry. McFarland called in the chase and Cruz flipped on the siren. The Cadillac turned left on McHenry with smoke boiling from the tires, almost hitting a teenage boy and girl on their way home from the theater.

"He's gonna kill someone driving like that," Cruz said, slowing as he entered the intersection.

******

Curtis released a plethora of curses, glancing at the lights in the rearview mirror. He'd been stupid not to take Mindy's offer to call a taxi. Being cited for drunk driving was one sure way to kill a political career. He could have easily explained away Cindy and Elizabeth Sparks in a year or two. America's attention span was quite small. But not this. He had to get away.

Orangeburg Avenue was up ahead. Doctor's Medical Center was off Orangeburg. He could turn left on Orangeburg, then a quick right and ditch the car in the hospital parking lot.

He hit the break as Orangeburg appeared and cranked the steering wheel left. The Cadillac's tires squealed loudly as the S.U.V. slid lazily sideways. Curtis cranked the steering wheel to the right in an attempt to stop the slide and jumped the curb, where he ricocheted off a light pole and snapped the safety chain, plowing into two cars in the *Five Star Used Car* lot.

A second squad car pulled across McHenry Ave. blocking traffic as Cruz called for an ambulance. One of the officers from the second car was lighting flares.

"Curtis Roberts," McFarland said, prying open the driver's door.

"That's who it is?" Cruz said.

"Yeah. I've seen him up close a couple of times."

Cruz chuckled as he took a closer look at Curt's face. Blood was pouring from his already broken nose. "He's really having a bad year, isn't he?"

The ambulance turned the corner as the wail from a firetruck drew closer.

"Well, if you're gonna get tanked and wreck a car, you couldn't pick a better spot than a block from a hospital." McFarland peeked through the driver's window as Curtis moaned. "Hang on, Curt. The ambulance is here and the so is the fire truck. They'll get you out shortly."

******

Cindy wheeled her chair into the crowded ICU waiting room. The first call about the accident had come from Bobby who happened to be on duty and had arrived at the accident scene in a third squad car to help control traffic on McHenry Avenue. The second call came from Peter who had been on loan to Doctor's Medical Center due to a shortage of doctors in their ICU. He had been the attending physician when Curtis arrived. Visiting Curtis was not really high on her list of things to do, but seeing as they had once been friends, and seeing as they had once been engaged…sort of…she had been engaged even if he hadn't…she thought visiting him in the hospital would be the Christian thing to do. Zoe had arrived at the ranch early that morning to visit and insisted on accompanying them to the hospital.

"You guys wait here and I'll try to find out where he is and if we can see him," Edith said.

Cindy backed her chair close to the wall, where Steven

and Zoe took up residence flanking her. The wait took about ten minutes before Edith returned and heaved a deep sigh.

"Well, he's currently in X-ray, and they'll only let two people in at a time, and preferably family."

"So, we might not get to see him at all?" Steven said.

"Maybe not."

"All I wanted to do was pray for him and…"

She was interrupted by a screech as Darlene Roberts, Curtis' mother, charged across the room releasing a string of profanities.

"What are you doing here? Get out! Get out! All of you. Haven't you done enough to my boy? Now you're here to gloat over him when he's hurt."

Warren, Curtis' father, tried restraining her, but she fought him off and wound up trapping Cindy against the wall. Zoe almost leaped across Cindy in an effort to protect her friend. Steven grabbed Zoe around the waist when she got in Darlene's face with clenched fists.

"Hold on there, cowgirl," Steven growled, lifting her off her feet. He almost carried her outside where she wiggled from his grip and made another try for the door.

"No, you don't want to be in there right now," Steven said as he pulled Zoe back through the door.

"You've got that wrong," she said in a loud voice. "I'm gonna rearrange her face."

"Yeah, I know, but that'd make you just a bad as her. Leave her alone."

"But…"

"Cindy and Edith are going to be okay. See?" Steven pulled her away from the door. Several men and women had crowded around Cindy and Edith, shielding them from Darlene and helped them through the door.

"Okay, okay," Zoe said, waving him off.

Steven turned to thank the people who helped Cindy and Edith when Zoe slipped back inside. He growled and yelled for her to get back outside, but relaxed as Zoe pulled her smart phone from her hip pocket and videoed a security guard trying to restrain Darlene Roberts. Zoe looked as though she was finished, when Darlene hit the security guard and he slapped a pair of handcuffs on her wrists. Zoe grinned and took a couple more photographs as a Modesto police officer guided Darlene toward a waiting police car.

******

"Well, that's an exciting way to start the day," Edith said and took a sip of coffee. They were seated in a corner booth at I-Hop waiting for breakfast before returning to the ranch. "I guess we know who Curt takes after."

"You can say that again," Steven snickered. "I thought I was gonna have to hog tie Zoe there for a minute. What got you so riled, anyway?"

"What got me riled? You heard what she said. No one's gonna call one of my friends, especially Cindy, those names and get away with it. I thought you would've gotten ticked-off too."

"Well, I wasn't too pleased, if that's what's eating at your craw. I just didn't know you had all that spit and vinegar inside you. That's all."

Cindy laid a warm hand on Zoe's arm. "Thanks, but you didn't need to do that. If you would have hit her, or even grabbed her, she would have filed a complaint and had you arrested, then, sued you. That wouldn't have been a good wedding present for Fred."

"What do you plan on doing with those pictures you took?" Steven asked.

"I don't know. I thought maybe Rita Lorenzo might want to see them."

"That's what I thought," Steven said. "Better pray about it first. It might not be what God really wants you to do."

"Well," Zoe sat back and glared at her coffee mug on the table. "If she says a bunch of stuff about Cindy and us coming to the hospital…you'd better believe I'm going to give the flash-drive to Rita."

"Yes, that might change the rules, if that happens. But let's pray that doesn't happen," Edith said softly.

They looked up as Bobby walked in, still dressed in his uniform. Steven waved for him to join their table, which he did and the waitress set a coffee mug in front of him.

"Ah, just coffee. I've got to get home and corral two kids so my wife can get some rest."

"Good man," the waitress said with a grin. "Want to come and talk to my husband for me?"

"It's something born inside a man. Either he does it, or doesn't," Edith said. "It can't be taught."

"Please don't tell me that," she said and walked back toward the kitchen shaking her head.

"Boy, you ruined her day," Cindy said. "As a matter of fact, it didn't make me feel too good either."

"You? Why?" Edith said.

"Well, just for discussion sake, let's just say I did meet someone who I wanted to marry me, and we had a baby. I would need a little extra help, being stuck in this chair. Now, you're telling me my husband might not help me raise our child."

"Now I'm not so sure I wanna get married either," Zoe said.

"See what you caused, being so helpful around the house?" Steven said with a snort toward Bobby.

"Me? I didn't say anything. It was Mom who said it."

Chapter 54

"So, how have you been doing with your exercises at home?" Gloria asked as she led Cynthia and Edith into the therapy room.

"Cindy's been doing much better than I thought she would do," Edith said.

"Oh? Well maybe Cindy would like to tell me about it." Gloria sat on a stool and studied Cindy closely.

"I've actually gotten some feeling back into my legs."

"Really? Do both of them feel the same, or different?"

"My left leg has more feeling than the right, but the right leg has gotten a little feeling now. Not much, but some."

"That's because there was more nerve damage on one side than the other. What does it feel like?"

Tingly, like my whole leg is asleep."

"Will that ever go away?" Edith asked.

"Maybe," Gloria said. "I've seen it happen, but it can take years. One man I worked with fell off a house and broke his wrist bad enough to require pins. He lost the feeling in that hand. It took three years, but the feeling eventually returned."

Gloria collected the ball from the bin and stood in front of Cindy.

"Now, today we're going to play a different game. I want you to sit on the walker facing me." She waited while Edith helped Cindy get situated.

"Okay, now I want you to kick the ball, using whatever foot I say. Okay?" Gloria held the ball toward

Cindy and shouted. "Left foot!"

Cindy tried but got nothing.

"Okay, calm down," she said as Cindy started getting frustrated. "You're thinking too much. Um, let me see." She turned her back toward Cindy for a few seconds, then turned quickly and shouted. "Right foot." Cindy's right foot moved a few inches.

"See? You might not have kicked the ball, but you moved your right leg. Let's try it again." She turned her back on Cindy, then quickly turned and yelled. "Left foot!"

Edith and Gloria both clapped and cheered as she kicked the ball from Gloria's hands. "See? I told you, you're thinking way too much. Your body's healing very well. It's mostly up here in your head right now." Gloria tapped Cindy on the side of her head.

"So, what the shrink said is true? I am crazy?"

"Well, we're all crazy to one degree or the other," Gloria said as she retrieved the ball. "And since we're all nuts, let's have some fun."

Gloria turned her back on Cindy again, then turned and shouted. "Right foot!"

Cindy's right leg moved enough to kick the ball without knocking it from her hands.

"Very good, Cindy. Very good. That deserves a milkshake on your way home."

Chapter 55

Peter glanced at the clock before changing into his Levis and boots. He had just finished pulling a double back-to-back shift and should be in bed, but the saving of a ten-year-old girl's life had him keyed up, and he knew sleep would come later.

He stopped at a twenty-four hour coffee shop and purchased a huge Styrofoam cup of black coffee and drove to the ranch. He had saddled Buster and walked him past the corral by the time the sun began to peek over the mountains to the east. Peter climbed into the saddle and set the pace at a gentle trot toward the fall pasture. He spent the next two hours walking Buster around the herd for no reason, and allowing his mind to wander aimlessly.

The sun was high and had begun to warm the chill off the night air when his father galloped up to join him.

"Seth said you were here. Care for a little company?"

"I was hoping for some quiet to get things sorted out inside my head."

"Yeah," Steven snickered, "things got kind of messy there for a minute."

"Yeah, I suppose they did."

Peter slid out of the saddle and pretended to check the cinches.

Steven dismounted also and pulled a thermos of coffee from his saddle bag and filled two cups.

"Well, I promise not to bug you too much. Here," he handed one of the cups to Peter. "Drink this. Made it myself. It's a little stronger than your ma's. Maybe it will clear the cobwebs out of your head."

He waited until Peter had taken a couple of sips.

"You haven't been to the house or said more'n two words to Cindy since Curt's meltdown. What's going on?"

"We've been swamped at the hospital. I pulled a double shift, and haven't slept in so long I've forgotten how." Peter glanced at his father. "I started to call her several times, but I don't know what to say."

"How about saying you're sorry she got hurt and that you'll always be there? That's a good place to start."

Peter kicked at a dirt clod and turned his gaze toward the clouds.

"I told her about him a couple of times when he first started calling and asking her out. I warned her way back in high school when she got her first crush on him. Then, I tried to warn her about getting involved in his campaign but she wouldn't listen. In a way, she got what she deserved."

Steven tossed the contents of his cup on the ground and glared at his son.

"Well, that may be so. But we'd all be in a heap of trouble if we got what we deserved, now wouldn't we? You're not the victim here. That girl back at the house is. She got crippled defending our country, and then she was made a national laughing stock by a man who gave her a ring and said he loved her."

Steven stuffed the thermos and mug back in the saddlebag and mounted his horse then turned back to glare once again at Peter.

"You've somehow made this whole thing about yourself, but it's not about you. It's about her. You'd best quit feeling sorry for yourself. Get on your knees and do a little soul-searching, boy."

Peter watched as his father rode away before taking another sip of coffee. He looked at the contents of the cup and tossed it. He then glanced at the sky before kneeling beside the rotting log.

"Okay God, I'm sorry. Dad's right. I'm angry at her

and bitter. Please, you've got to help me, because I can't do this on my own. So, tell me what you want me to do."

******

Cindy watched the familiar figure through the living room window as he rode Buster into the yard and dismounted next to the corral. He unsaddled and turned the sorrel loose inside the corral and carried the saddle inside the barn. Watching him, she realized just how much she missed him. She missed the sound of his voice, his smell when he had been riding, his laugh—she missed Peter Fowler. Besides, she wanted to tell him the news that she had walked the length of the therapy room and back again using the walker. It was true that the therapist had held onto her belt, but he was right—she could walk, placing one foot in front of the other. She felt her heartbeat pick up speed and she checked her reflection in the glass, waiting for him to reappear from the barn and come to the house.

Steven and Edith came from the tack house and almost bumped into Peter as he stepped from the shadows inside the barn. Peter hugged both parents and then the three of them chatted for what seemed an eternity. Cindy couldn't hear a word from this distance, especially from inside the house, so she cracked the window open in desperation, but to no avail. She still couldn't hear.

Finally, after deciding she was fighting a losing battle, she wheeled her chair around and headed toward the door. That was when Peter gave both parents another hug and walked briskly toward his truck. She opened the door and inched her chair onto the porch, thinking maybe he had simply gone to retrieve something from the truck, only to feel her heart explode inside her chest as Peter started the truck and drove away.

Chapter 56

Cindy cradled her forehead against her palm and stared at the ledger. It had been three days since seeing Peter outside the barn, and an ever-increasing stack of bills and paper was piled in one corner of the desk. No matter how hard she tried, Cindy couldn't focus on the mess lying in front of her. She glanced up as Peter entered the front door and grinned.

"Still haven't given up yet?"

Cynthia returned her focus back to the desk.

"Huh? Ah...no. Not yet. Getting close, but not quite there yet."

"You're tougher than I thought."

He smiled at her once more and walked briskly into the kitchen. Cynthia stared at the kitchen door for a few seconds, shrugged, then returned to staring at the ledger. She turned her attention back to the kitchen when she heard Peter and his mother start talking.

"What are you doing?" Edith's voice sounded irritated.

"Making sandwiches."

"I just cleaned this kitchen. You should have been here earlier, if you're hungry. I fixed sausage, eggs, biscuits and gravy for breakfast."

"Yeah, I know. Dad climbed my ladder for not coming around, but we've been busy at the hospital. Besides, this isn't for breakfast. This is for a picnic."

"Picnic?"

"Yeah, a picnic."

The sound of clinking and fumbling inside the refrigerator floated out of the kitchen door.

"Here," Edith snapped. "You're going to make a mess. I'll pack your lunch. Just get out of my kitchen."

Peter came into the living room then poked his head back into the kitchen.

"Thanks, Ma. You're the best."

"I know how great I am. Just get!"

Peter left the kitchen and walked slowly in a half circle as he studied Cindy from head to toe.

"The jeans and tennis shoes are fine, but you'll need a hat and jacket. It's kind of cool outside, and there are clouds blowing in."

Cindy shrugged her shoulders and turned her attention back to the ledger.

"Doesn't sound like a good day for a picnic. You might get rained on."

"It'll be worth it. It's the perfect day for one. Come on…" He grabbed the handles on the wheelchair and wheeled her to the center of the living room.

"Hey! What do you think you're doing? I promised your dad I'd finish the bookkeeping today."

"Dad wouldn't notice either way. You can always finish the bookkeeping later."

"I'm not going," Cindy yelled as Peter grabbed her jacket and hat from the coat closet.

"Think of it as a present to me," Edith said, placing a paper grocery bag on the dining room table. "Please, get him out of the house before he makes a big mess."

******

The buggy rolled easily down the dirt field road at a fast trot. Peter felt a twinge of guilt, realizing he hadn't been to the ranch in over a week, and Pedro had more than likely not been exercised. He made a mental promise to the horse that would not happen again.

He looked at the silent woman seated beside him and grinned. She had the hat pulled low and her arms crossed across her breasts. She hadn't said a single word since leaving the house.

"I take it you're mad at me over something."

She kept the rigid pose without uttering a word. Peter guided the buggy off the road and came to a halt under a massive oak tree. A homemade swing dangled from one of the bigger branches.

Cindy's head rose as she eyed the swing. She turned her eyes to Peter, then back to the swing.

"A swing? Did you do that?"

"Uh-huh," he said with a nod. "I know how you used to love to swing."

Peter filled two mugs with coffee from a thermos as Cynthia began snooping inside the grocery bag.

"I still like to swing…I just can't."

She quit rummaging in the bag and looked up, holding two sandwiches and smiled.

"She packed peanut butter and grape jelly sandwiches, like when we were in grade school. You have the greatest mother in the world."

"Yeah, I know we do."

Peter sat his coffee aside and climbed out. He rounded the buggy to stand by Cindy and held out his arms.

"Come here."

"Why, what are you doing?"

"I'm going to swing you."

"Ah…I don't know about that. I might fall out of that thing."

"You won't. I promise."

He placed Cindy in the swing and took his time belting her in. "I read about a girl in Utah who loves horses and competed in barrel racing. She had her spinal cord severed in an automobile accident, and was paralyzed from the waist down, much like you…only worse. She couldn't feel a thing. Anyway, they added a seatbelt to her saddle and she's back competing in barrel racing once again. I'm thinking we should try that with you." He snugged the belt and smiled.

"So, tell me, how have you been holding up? We haven't spoken much the past few weeks."

"We haven't spoken at all. I thought you were mad at me for some reason."

Peter shook his head.

"No, I was angry at Curt for what he did. And, I guess I was a little put out that you allowed yourself to be used. But not at you. Fact is, I owe you an apology. "

"Really? What for?" Cindy said.

"I promised to be there when you needed me, and I wasn't. To tell the truth, I did get angry and bitter watching you kiss Curt. I'm really sorry."

"Apology accepted." Cindy's voice was almost a whisper. "I'm sorry too."

Peter gave another tug on the belt, then gently pushed the swing while facing her.

Cindy glanced around her as the swing rose higher.

"This really is a beautiful ranch. I could die here and be happy."

Peter pushed the swing higher.

"I know this is going to sound crazy for a man to ask, but do you ever think about when we were kids?"

"Yeah," she said with a weak smile. "Quite frequently. Why?"

"Me too. I remember sitting in Miss William's kindergarten class the day she introduced you as a new student and seated you next to me. You were a skinny little thing, and when you smiled, you were missing your front teeth. You were wearing a white dress with blue and pink flowers, and the toes of your shoes were scuffed."

Cindy's eyes watered as she choked out, "You remember that?"

Peter stopped the swing and studied her face.

"Yes. I took one look at you, and knew you were the

prettiest girl I had ever seen."

A tear escaped her watery eyes and mapped its way down her cheek.

"I fell in love with you that day, and I've never stopped."

He took both of her hands and studied them.

"Cindy, I'm not a good speaker like Curt, and I don't always say the right things. And I know my timing stinks, but I'll never hurt you. Will you marry me?"

She burst into tears and covered her face with both hands before punching him in the arm soundly.

"Ow! What was that for?"

"You rat! Why didn't you tell me? I wouldn't have looked at Curt if I'd known."

She half-laughed and half-cried as she threw her arms around his neck. "Yes, I'll marry you! I don't deserve you, but I'll marry you, if you really want me."

"I've always wanted you Cindy."

She kissed him repeatedly on his lips and cheeks then stopped as lightning flashed across the sky, followed by a deep roll of thunder. The wind changed direction as the first drops fell. Pedro released a whinny at a second clap of thunder and turned the buggy in a tight circle and galloped toward the barn.

"Think that's an omen?" Peter said and burst into laughter.

"What do we do now?" she said, wiping her wet hair from her eyes.

"Call mom like we've done all our lives."

Peter pulled his cell phone from his pocket and began punching numbers. She answered on the third ring.

"Mom? Yeah, we need you to come get us. Pedro spooked and left us stranded. We're on the road to the winter range. Yeah, thanks, Mom."

"Is she coming?"

"Yes, she said she'd be here as soon as she can."

"Now what?" Cindy asked.

"We wait for her." He grinned at her. "We can finish what we started while we're waiting."

She wrapped her arms around his neck as she kissed him again.

The Valley of Decision

******

Steven chuckled as he idled the truck. They were parked on a small hill approximately an eighth of a mile from where Peter and Cindy were. The heater was keeping the cab toasty, and the young couple had to be freezing.

"Maybe we should rescue them now."

"Wait just a minute longer," Edith said as she adjusted the telescoping lends on her camera. She had a feeling the picnickers were going to get wet the moment they left the house. She called Steven and asked him to bring the four-wheel drive truck as she packed dry towels and plastic bags for muddy shoes. They had passed the buggy going the opposite way a quarter of a mile back, and followed the road slowly, keeping out of sight when possible, giving the young couple some privacy.

"Think they'll always need our help?" Steven looked at her slantwise.

"Mmm, maybe. As much as we'll allow, anyway."

The camera in her hand clicked twice more.

"Okay, let's go rescue them."

End

Thank You

We sincerely hope you enjoyed reading The Valley of Decision. Please visit our website for other books written by this author.

Poverty Flat
A Reason to Believe
Canyon Wind

The Doña Series
The Doña
Mokelumne Gold

The Manhunter Series
Manhunter
Where The Green Grass Grows

The Dusty Boots Series
Dusty Boots
Joker's Play
Refugio's Gold
Cool Water Justice

Children's Books
The Witch on Oak Street
Charlie Shepherd
I'm Molly

MAJOR MITCHELL is the author of nine historical westerns, two contemporary novels and three children's books. He lives with his wife, Judy, in Northern California. He is a member of The Western Writers of America and a frequent guest speaker at historical meetings and schools on the west coast. He has also written several songs, and takes the stage on rare occasions as a singer.

www.ingramcontent.com/pod-product-compliance
Lightning Source LLC
Chambersburg PA
CBHW021059080526
44587CB00010B/303